MODERN CHRISTIAN REVOLUTIONARIES SERIES

General Editor:
DONALD ATTWATER

NATHAN SÖDERBLOM: A PROPHET OF CHRISTIAN UNITY

He who praises a man ought to follow him, and if he be not ready to follow him he ought not to praise him.—*St. John Chrysostom.*

MODERN CHRISTIAN REVOLUTIONARIES

NATHAN SÖDERBLOM: A PROPHET OF CHRISTIAN UNITY

By the Reverend
PETER KATZ, PH.D.

WITH SELECTIONS FROM THE MEMORIAL WRITINGS
OF BISHOP BERGGRAV, BISHOP BRILIOTH, BISHOP
ANDRAE AND OTHERS, AND AN INTRODUCTION BY
THE BISHOP OF CHICHESTER

> When ye shall have done all those things which are commanded you, say: We are unprofitable servants; we have done that which was our duty to do.—*St. Luke's Gospel*, xvii, 10.

WIPF & STOCK · Eugene, Oregon

Wipf and Stock Publishers
199 W 8th Ave, Suite 3
Eugene, OR 97401

Nathan Söderblom
A Prophet of Christian Unity
By Katz, Peter
Copyright©1949 James Clarke Lutterworth Press
ISBN 13: 978-1-5326-8609-2
Publication date 3/22/2019
Previously published by James Clarke & Co. LTD., 1949

PREFACE

THE nations of Scandinavia, the descendants of the Vikings, still from time to time send out world-conquerors of an increasingly spiritualized type. For centuries the name of Gustavus Adolphus, the saviour of continental Protestantism, has stood out, and we must go back to him to find the proper standards of comparison for a figure like Nathan Söderblom, himself a real "defender of the faith." His great name stands for a great cause. Already the ranks of his champions begin to grow thinner, but there are still many at work who received a decisive impulse from him: for them the saga of Nathan Söderblom, inspiring their loftiest thoughts and achievements, is no story of the past. So the following pages will be neither hagiography nor a monograph for experts, but directed to the wider circle of those for whom the struggle for church reunion, social peace, and international good-will forms an important part of their spiritual life.

After Söderblom's death an abundance of memorial literature appeared: biographies (1),[1] memoirs (2), and a first volume giving a competent analysis of his thought and achievement (3). Later on, research began to take the place of memoirs and immediate impressions: documents which illustrate his development have been published (4), and also a monograph of great importance dealing with the central problems with which he wrestled throughout his life (5). This literature, written mainly in the Scandinavian languages, is necessarily hidden treasure to those unfamiliar with northern tongues; and the majority of foreign contributors can no longer understand their articles after they have been printed in Swedish. It therefore seems appropriate to

[1] The figures refer to items in the bibliography.

try to give an idea of what is best among these thousands of pages; and, since this literature has been written for a Swedish public and the readers of the present survey speak English, I quote the major portion of Bishop Berggrav's study, which Söderblom's Danish biographer considers "a jewel of writing." Not being Swedish in temperament, he gives us a picture at once intimate and independent (pp. 11–30). I add selections in appreciation of Söderblom's importance as a religious historian and as a theologian, and, in greater fulness, as a champion of the oecumenical ideal (pp. 31–51).To complete the picture of his oecumenical activities I then point out that Söderblom set about solving the problem of reunion by getting the various churches to collaborate in immediate practical tasks of social (pp. 52–66) and international (pp. 67–76) importance, so as to draw them closer together as they approached the goal of their common endeavours. Finally I attempt the necessary, though difficult, task of reproducing what is most valuable in the abundance of the personal memorial literature (pp. 77–92). Having ventured to write a modest monograph on Söderblom's life and work as early as 1925 (6), and a brief survey of his literary production after his death (7), this time I confine myself to the function of what the Gospel calls "a faithful steward."

I should like to take this opportunity of expressing my thanks to my friend the Reverend J. N. Sanders, who has spent much time and shown great patience in correcting many of the grosser blunders in my rather faulty English.

P. K.

INTRODUCTION

NATHAN SÖDERBLOM was born at Trönö on January 15th, 1866, and died at Uppsala on July 12th, 1931. He was a man of many gifts. Not only was he a master in the history of religion, an inspired teacher of the Christian religion, and in particular a great interpreter of Luther; but he was a fine spiritual guide, a true father-in-God to his diocese, and an eloquent preacher and speaker; and he was also a lover of music and literature, expert in many languages, and rejoicing in a multitude of friends. Yet these are only some of the elements which helped to make him a modern Christian revolutionary. The quality which distinguished him above all his contemporaries was a consuming passion for Christian unity, and a determination to spend all the strength he had in helping to bring the churches at least one step further forward to that goal.

He succeeded to the office of archbishop of Uppsala in 1914. His appointment by the King of Sweden was a general surprise, for he was the last on the list of nominations presented according to law by the church and university authorities. But almost immediately after his election, at the beginning of the first world war, he initiated an appeal for peace and fellowship, which was in effect a confession of Christian unity in spite of war, and a summons to keep the thought of peace alive. It was signed by a number of influential church leaders from neutral countries, and by the Archbishop of Finland and Bishop Ferencz, of Hungary. He had exceptional qualifications for the role of a mediator where Christians of different nations were concerned. He had played a leading part in the theological conferences between the Church of England and the Church of Sweden in 1909, which ultimately led to intercommunion. He had also been chaplain in Paris from 1894 to 1901, before becoming professor of the history of religion in Uppsala (1901-14); and he occupied the same chair simultaneously for two years at Leipzig University (1912-14), living in Leipzig for half of each year.

His appeal in 1914 was not destined to prevail. Undeterred, he sought to convene an international Christian conference in the middle of the war, but had to be satisfied with a conference of Christians from Scandinavian countries only, in 1917. It was however in October 1919, when at last the church leaders of most belligerent countries (except France) met together at Oud Wassenaar in Holland under the auspices of the World Alliance for promoting International Friendship through the Churches, that he had the first great opportunity for winning a hearing for his appeal for Christian unity across the frontiers of nations. In that cause he spent himself until he died. The high-water mark of his activities was the Universal Christian Conference on Life and Work at Stockholm in 1925. The various accounts which follow in this book give a vivid impression of the untiring energy with which he worked, of the genius of the man himself, and of the nature of his achievement. I do not want to trespass on the territory so admirably covered by the author of this book, and by Bishops Berggrav, Brilioth, Tor Andrae, Aulén, and others, whose tributes Dr. Peter Katz brings together. But there are one or two things which I should like to stress.

The first quarter of the twentieth century was notable for the hopes and dreams, expressed in various ways, of a coming together of Christians of different communions. It saw the beginnings of world missionary co-operation, of the Student Christian Movement, of planning for a clearer understanding of the variations in faith and order between the different churches, of a movement for promoting international friendship through the churches. All these

INTRODUCTION

were favourable signs, though small enough in face of the growing antagonism of the nations. There were also great individual leaders in the international Christian field. I think especially of John R. Mott (of the Y.M.C.A. and the International Missionary Council); C. H. Brent, Bishop of the Philippine Islands and then of Western New York; Nikolai Velimirovic, Bishop of Ochrida; and Lord Robert Cecil. There were fine scholars with an international range, like Adolf Deissmann, of Berlin; and fine international church statesmen, like Archbishop Davidson. But none of these, great as they are, could have achieved what Söderblom achieved in the Stockholm Conference.

Söderblom's vision was not simply a statesman's vision, nor a prophet's vision, nor a missionary's vision. It was the vision of a churchman, born of the very tribulation of war, who, accepting the churches as they are and without attempting to adjust or reconcile their creeds or their ministries, was driven on by faith in the Universal Church, and desired to see the existing churches crossing the frontiers of nations and races and classes, and binding their members together in a universal Christian fellowship. He knew that he could not get even the beginning of this, unless he was able to make the churches see a panorama of such a fellowship in a concrete and living form. Hence his determination to achieve the Stockholm Conference. He had many setbacks: he had to wait longer than he had hoped: and he had to persuade men of many churches and countries that the idea was not a wild dream and that the plan itself was sound. He was helped much by the Church Peace Union in U.S.A., and by the World Alliance for promoting International Friendship through the Churches. By one means or another he gathered helpers about him, partly through old international connexions, partly through a following up of the efforts he had made in war time, partly through the warm encouragement of numerous Swedish friends, when the place of meeting was finally chosen. But it is quite certain that, so far as human factors are concerned, it was Söderblom's courage, unfailing vitality and humour, and his boundless faith in Christian unity, that brought the Conference to birth, and gave such powerful testimony to the truth that in a bitterly divided world the Cross stands, for all who will see it, as the great uniting force. The Conference was only a beginning, as the message with which it ended made clear. Between 1925 and 1946 many new things in thought and action have come about. But it was largely through Söderblom's influence that the word 'oecumenical' obtained its present place in the language of the Church. And it was the Stockholm Conference and its sequel, the Universal Christian Council for Life and Work, that gave the first great impetus to the World Council of Churches, now the official permanent instrument of co-operation between the churches in the social and international field, and meeting in full assembly in 1948. I am confident that, when the history of the first half of the twentieth century comes to be written, it will be Nathan Söderblom who will stand out as the man who did more than any other Christian leader or teacher to unite Orthodox and Evangelical churches of all nations and communions in a common fellowship, for the sake of Christ, and His truth and justice and peace.

GEORGE CICESTR:

Uppsala,
  October, 1946

1

BISHOP EIVIND BERGGRAV of Oslo does not give a biography but presupposes a knowledge of the facts of Söderblom's life. He takes as his text the assertion of an Oslo newspaper obituary, which he says is as misleading as can be: it runs thus: "The secret of Söderblom is, above all, that the archbishop was a simple and happy man." Berggrav thinks that this view of Söderblom as living his life in the pure sunshine of unbroken success was "dreadfully untrue." From his earliest years Söderblom experienced deep religious crises; first when he witnessed his father's struggle to break through from the fear of the law to the gospel of freedom—a struggle which led him to the verge of insanity; secondly at the university, where he encountered "modern" views. "This is no 'simple' situation." Söderblom did not shun these difficulties, but fought his way through the problems and became a leader in overcoming them.

"In truth he always remained a son of the Evangelical Revival, which occurred in Sweden a century ago, without ever becoming its servant. This free-born spirit of adoption gives his theology its line. Christianity in his mind never was in need of being 'defended' against other religions. On the contrary, he believed it to be the source from which other religions receive such truth as they possess, like dew-drops which derive their radiance from the light of the sun.

"And this radiance of Christianity did not originate from the high moral idealism of Jesus. No; the main thing was the specifically *religious* element in the whole complex which makes up Christianity. It was here that Söderblom broke new ground in opposition to

Ritschlianism. In what Delitzsch called the 'Babel *versus* Bible controversy,' when he tried to use evidence from Babylonian sources to impugn the trustworthiness of the Old Testament, his opponents attempted to save Christianity by emphasizing that it stood so high ethically. No, said Söderblom; it is just the other way round; the central thing is the saving belief in Christ and his work. It is in virtue of this belief that Christianity *stands*. And so he made a comprehensive classification of all religions into two main types, as 'religions of *revelation*' and 'religions of *culture*,' the latter of which he regarded as not merely inferior to the former, but almost as outside of comparison with it. The religions of culture follow the development of culture, determined by it instead of determining it. They are thus always in accordance with their time, they are 'moral' and 'modern,' they are religions of the state, religions of compromise. On higher intellectual and cultural levels they easily disintegrate into pantheism and idealism. Therefore, according to Söderblom, they are not religions in the proper sense of the word. For, he says, the final question put to religion is not, 'How will you shape my life?' but 'Can you rescue my life and sustain it?' The religions which answer this question he calls 'religions of revelation,' because they rest on a message from eternity. They are also called prophetic religions, because the message from God is mediated through persons whom he claims wholly for himself, making them his instruments. This type he found only in Persia and Israel: in Zoroaster to a limited degree, and fully in Moses and the prophets. The religions of revelation are not the product of human environment nor are they a 'psychic vibration.' They proceed from God's own intervention and communication through his human instruments and through history. And here Christ is not merely the culminating point, but the realization of that at which the others had only hinted.

"Therefore Söderblom excluded from genuine religion all 'haziness' and ecstasy resting on a heightening of merely human emotion. This he called 'mysticism of infinity.' At its highest it is ecstasy, the extinction of the self, the effacement of personality and responsibility. To this he opposed the 'mysticism of personality.' Here blossoms all that is highest in the spiritual life of the individual—full responsibility, great concentration of vision and powers, but at the same time something beyond words, something indefinable. In spite of Ritschl and Herrmann, Söderblom retained the word 'mysticism,' because he gave such emphasis to the specifically religious, always holding that in the communion of faith with God there is something 'mysterious': actual contact with God. And where the relation to God is based upon personal contact and has a historical and ethical orientation, it bears within itself some secret of its own.

"This differentiation between the religiosity of culture and the religion of revelation or, on the other hand, between losing one's personality in infinity and winning it through belief, meant a break through to new central standards of valuation and gave a new stimulus to very many scholars. Now there was no longer any need to look anxiously for a place for Christianity: it just stood! If religion is tested solely by answering the question, Can it release me from being engulfed in sin, meaninglessness and desperation?— then Christ himself comes forth as the sole revelation; we apprehend him, because he has already apprehended us. 'The centre of my theology is the mystery of the vicarious passion of Christ.'" Berggrav is aware that he can only give "a cross-section through the central layer of Söderblom's scientific achievements; but all the same it shows how throughout his life, from childhood onwards, he was continually oscillating between contradictory positions right up to his final theological synthesis. This latter was not, however, the result of any faculty of versatile accommodation, but to the last it remained oscillating and full of tensions. He who with the clearest insight declared culture to be something secondary, and even a possible danger to the very life of religion—he who (as everyone knows) not only loved culture but, one may say, 'practised' it, doing homage to it and sharing it with artists, men of letters, diplomats, socialists—he did not live a double life, fraternizing with the enemy and warming himself between whiles at their hearth. He felt the need ever afresh to emphasize the 'centre.' . . . Only he did not need to have his centre of gravity in details, because he had it so decidedly, so dominatingly in his inmost heart. He believed in God, and so he was free. Where others wavered, he stood unshaken. The whole life of culture was to him personally not a danger but a possibility. How could he take up a really central position in the epoch in which God had placed him, and in which he had received God's revelation? He felt at one with much that in the present time was good, inquiring and healthy and, what is more, he appreciated what 'our time' means for every time and every generation. He loved men—but not because he relied upon them and trusted in their nature. Yet where was all that which welled up in him to flow if not out to men, men as they were and as they resembled himself? He felt at home in the midst of the throng. It was for him simply the natural circumference of the circle of which his heart was the centre. Thus in relation to his own time he was never as the circumference to the centre, but always as the radius to the circumference, literally radiating towards it. . . . Whether there be culture or no—that makes no difference in itself: man and man's heart is the main thing. It was against the unhealthy kind of culture which like Moloch devours its own children that he struggled so passionately. To it he opposed Christ, the bringer of scandal and redemption.

"The agonies of a man who has 'entered into his closet' to pray do not concern the public. But their echo is sometimes perceptible in his words. The stronger we are ourselves, the greater must be God's impact upon us. And Söderblom's strength was strength indeed; it was continually coming back, even after God had conquered, for he had the energy of a giant. Who of us knows anything about his neighbour? Who of us knows what the greatest among us have deep within themselves? Who of us knows what demon has been given for the religious genius to wrestle with, precisely in that which gives him his radiance in the eyes of men? Hidden depths! Luther reveals something of it. And Söderblom loved Luther; yes, and more than loved: he suffered and struggled with him. If geniuses create the simplest things of all, that does not mean that their creation is equally simple: it is out of the deepest springs that the clearest waters well up. Perhaps this was why those who only saw Söderblom from a distance could apply to him the word 'simple.' A friend asks, 'Whence came the immense inner force which was the mystery of his nature?' And he replies 'From a confident and living faith in God. His was a personality revealing in heart and life a power and nature overcoming transience and bearing in itself eternity.' A vanquished socialist adversary adds, 'He revealed Christ.'"

"Happy"? In the commonest of its many meanings the word is badly out of place here. Berggrav saw this, and tells us how disillusioned was the public, which since the Stockholm conference had been awaiting some unexpectedly brilliant literary achievement from Söderblom, when he published his book about the passion of Christ. "Was it with such things that he was concerned at the precise moment when such a triumph had fallen to his lot?"

Nevertheless, "the suffering Christ was his saviour in his own suffering, when everything else was wrecked. Here Söderblom did not simply hold a theory or an idea. He had a cross of his own. All that need be said is that Söderblom had the gift of sharing another's suffering in too high a degree to stand on his own defence when the agonies of people comparatively remote overwhelmed him with crushing violence. His path, which from afar seemed strewn with roses, was not seldom beset with thorns, and for the man with bare feet thorns are not the same thing as for the man with a good pair of shoes. Söderblom's vulnerability was due to his guileless nature, his good faith in men. He held out a warm hand—and men held out to him a cold one. He did not become a sceptic for that; he did not even become distrustful enough. As Bishop Ammundsen says, 'He showed an unusual generosity towards his adversaries. If he was given an opportunity of hitting back, he preferred to let it pass and to do them a good turn.' He was even prepared to say that he was grateful for public criticism, since it gave him the opportunity of explaining himself better. The old suspicions that Söderblom was unorthodox were always being stirred up afresh by his colleague the aged Archbishop of Åbo, whose strictures were based on his onesided eschatological views derived from J. T. Beck, of Tübingen.

These suspicions were seized upon eagerly and from a variety of motives by many a Lutheran paper and—as their anxiety to refute him grew—by the Roman Catholic press throughout the world. A priest of his own church published a scurrilous novel against him, full of ingenious lies and infamies. Ammundsen says that 'This mistrust of his orthodoxy was behind all the attacks made against him.' Söderblom was no politician, and for that reason the more vulnerable and defenceless.

" 'Simple and happy': so he was in his home, as a host, and there are many who keep this picture of him in grateful remembrance. Sorrow and tribulation could not blight him, and he throws light upon the source of his happiness when he says: 'The greatest grace I implore for the hour of my death is that the figure of Jesus crucified may stand before my inner vision, and that neither pain nor exhaustion may obscure it.' 'And all these things shall be added unto you.' Thus, in spite of all, he returned to his friends out of his 'closet,' where God alone knew what he had shared with him, like a new-born sun. This sun had a spectrum as richly graduated as can be only if the noblest and most manifold abilities have been melted down in the furnace kindled by the Creator. And we others were allowed to enjoy the radiant colours without being obliged to give a thought to the fact that in the refining fire the flame of suffering was one of the strongest. The grievous bodily pains of his later years were but a further preparation for the radiance of his last hours."

§

After having thus laid the foundations by a profound psychological analysis, Berggrav goes on to define more and more closely the problems raised by this analysis:

"What was the inmost nature of Söderblom, the peculiar mystery of his success? In what is his greatness, his genius, to be perceived?"

At the time of his surprising election to the archbishopric of Uppsala nobody could know the degree to which his inner equipment and the special way along which he had been led enabled him to fill his position as he did—and did still more adequately when war and its issues enlarged his task. Nobody knew that the man who (like almost all oecumenical leaders) had been an active member of the Student Christian Movement, had already perceived in 1890, when he was twenty-four years old and attending the student conference at Northfield, U.S.A., "a powerful impression of the unity of the church of Christ" and had written in his diary the prophetic prayer, "O Lord, give me humility and wisdom to serve the great cause of the free unity of thy church."

> "Only the future could make clear what it meant that the coming leader, as a minister in Paris (1894), a professor at Uppsala (1901) and at Leipzig (1912), had created a personal background for the task to come. His position required him to be, indeed, 'an Israelite, in whom is no guile.' The Lord saw him under the figtree: 'Thou shalt see greater things than these.' So far the Bishop of Lund, in consecrating him, was right and a prophet. But when the war of 1914-18 brought into action all that he had been preparing in his quiet hours, his position also was necessary. Seen from outside, it was the unique combination of an archbishopric and a Nathan Söderblom which rendered the whole possible. Without the position he was too small for his task, and without him the position in itself was something still smaller. There are times and tasks which make the possession of a high position necessary, and there are

periods of fair weather in which it is as unnecessary as that of a pilot when a ship is in harbour.

"Was it Söderblom's genius or his character which made the whole possible? The answer will be again the same, but it must be given, for in general one is too quickly satisfied with saying that genius alone completed the task.

"In what then did his genius lie? The explanation is by no means simple. When lecturing he could give the impression of achieving a miracle of creation. But I came to the conviction that Söderblom would have been no more than a shining genius had his character not been chiselled out under the influence of Christ's passion. Whatever his blunders and weaknesses may have been, they were not merely part of his character, but they contributed as well to the greatness of his task and goal. Ashes have something to say about the fire, and in the forging of his character powerful elements had to be burnt away.

" 'Will' is an important word in his characterization. His sermons reveal him; he is fond of speaking about 'vocation and faithfulness'; he had given his pledge to God, and his vow had become a will of iron within him. He coined a new Swedish word meaning 'joy in responsibility.' In this there is an inheritance from his father, who was unswerving in the doing of his duty and had a strong will for self-denial. In the dictionary of duty the word 'in vain' does not exist.

"If the father was a hard worker, the son was destined to be that to a dangerous degree. No one could understand how he could keep on from morning till night. When I was designated to Tromsö, he sent me a copy of the minutes of three of his recent visitations. He meant to encourage and inspire me. I read half-way through the first one: it nearly made me giddy and—if

I imagined myself in the same situation—I would have been tempted to despair and to give up: meetings of all kinds from morning till night, conferences, invitations, and then sermons in three churches day after day! He must have had enormous energy, but I believe at least half of it consisted of the will to work. One thinks of his advice to the young priests he ordained: 'Remember that it is the intention of the Church that you shall work yourselves to death—but slowly!' He at any rate followed the first part of this. But work meant to him not merely getting things done. It was his life. He did not wish the ministers of the Church to rely merely on routine, on the security of the institution, on their assurance of employment. 'While every form of organized religion had disadvantages of its own, an established church is, I am afraid, such that one cannot count on all its ministers for electrifying spiritual power.' The day before he died, while his vigour was still undiminished, he drafted a plan for a revival campaign within the Church itself, and he intended to send out priests two and two together, 'able to support and to supplement each other whilst speaking and singing.' Their instructions ran, 'The main thing is to preach the gospel so as to win men's hearts. We shall pray for God's help that the walls by which men barricade themselves against the word of God may be demolished, so that the good tidings may go straight to their hearts.'

"All his thoughts and plans were rooted in his endeavour to show men the way to Heaven. But his eyes were open to the variety of types of men and to the riches of God, and so he never tried to save himself trouble by forcing men to take the conventional path, but he went out to meet them where they actually stood, and began from there. He allowed himself more time with a man than he ever did with a book. 'If you are too great to concern yourself with the smallest, you are too small to be a priest,' he said. That is the key of his winning contact with people. Söderblom saw in a group of people nothing less than a number of opportunities for personal contacts. He was never satisfied until he had succeeded in approaching each one individually. It is difficult for us others to understand how exacting that may have been, but he continued to achieve it until the last handshake of his life.

"Ordinary mortals seeing Söderblom in action involuntarily thought of the word 'restlessness.' Yes, many of us asked ourselves in the first years: "Is he not 'nervous'?" He was very lively from childhood. He could be seen presiding at a meeting and doing a dozen other things at the same time: but the remarkable thing was that he did not miss anything of what was said. His closing summary often gave much more point to what had been said than the speakers themselves had done. And at the same time he had his thought and care for everything else at meetings, whether in halls or churches. His brain swarmed! A continuous whirl of ideas and combinations, of discoveries and experiments —his notebook was often out even in church. And everything always had to be done, if possible, at once, especially if there was something he believed to be wrong, or something he could do to help some one.

" 'This cannot last,' we said to one another, when we saw him at the first church unity meeting in Uppsala in 1917, 'Such nervous restlessness will bring him to an untimely grave.' Yet that was certainly a wrong diagnosis. One cannot be 'nervous' for eighteen years of unceasing and comprehensive work, and yet achieve so much and keep so fully, not just abreast, but even ahead in research, culture, religion, administration. The results of the eighteen years are proof that it was not 'nervousness'—there ought to be a name found to describe the phenomenon which would lift it above the level of ordinary people like ourselves. He had a way of his own of being quiet. During the great communion service at the Stockholm meeting in 1925 my place in church was directly opposite to his. The administration of the sacrament alone took an hour and a half, and I thought this loss of time might be intolerable for him. But he sat in his chair more quietly than others, mostly with his hand at his head. When we went out he laid his arm round my shoulder and said, 'How beautiful is this rest in the presence of God.' It was as if he had read my thoughts and wished to teach me something. And from then onwards I saw a little of his 'mystery,' and it was not a thing which he had learnt in his later years. When opposition grew up after his designation to the archbishopric of Uppsala, Professor Rudin, the old mystic whose inner life Söderblom was to describe later on, answered it quietly in three words, 'Behold, he prayeth.'

"Ordinary 'nervous' people suffer from unrest about nothing, almost for unrest's sake. But Söderblom was always filled with something, and this caused his activity. Even if he only got a chair for an old woman in church, he did so 'with all his heart.' 'Nervousness' makes people concerned about themselves, but his activity was directed to the well-being of others. When he saw someone in a group who was a little out of touch, he intervened and helped. In the same way his thought flew round Europe, drawing out men. He could telegraph sunshine to people far away, so that they began to grow. But he was not self-sufficient, and what he looked for from others was not merely assistance, but advice and collaboration. When he pointed out something for one of us, it became a task which

we were anxious to carry out. It was in this way that
he kindled the zeal for unity in all the minds which had
felt the light of his personality shining on them during
the eleven years of preparation for the great Stockholm
meeting in 1925.

"It was his being so good which was the thing which
won men—not his social talents. The other day I compared what the leading labour journalist and politician
Arthur Engberg had said about him in 1919 with what
he said later on when he had made closer acquaintance
with Söderblom personally. His attack was reprinted
with pleasure (as often happened) by a conservative
pietist church paper, and it said that Söderblom was a
chameleon, showing all colours in a quick and deluding
change; no public figure in Sweden was a greater master
of the art of saying 'Yes' and 'No' at the same time;
he was a remarkable acrobat, one of our most excellent
actors, and so on . . . the whole thing bitingly ironical.
Engberg, as editor of the Stockholm paper *Socialdemokraten*, published the following obituary in 1931: 'It is as
if life has become poorer for me by the loss of him whom
I opposed so often and fought against time after time,
but whom I always admired and appreciated, and did
so more and more as the years passed. He was archbishop of the Swedish realm. He was the creator,
organizer and leader of the oecumenical movement. He
made the culture of Sweden known to the world, and
the culture of the world to Sweden. He was one of the
foremost in the movement for peace. But all these were
only brilliant outworks. It was his warm, fascinating,
enchanting personality, the child-like goodness of this
open and burning human soul, which won the victory.'
It is not men who are 'nervous' and preoccupied with
themselves who at last conquer others so completely.

"His greatness was not apparent to one looking at him

from afar—it became more obvious the closer one got to him. Söderblom, who could be the imposing prelate on occasion, was actually an unassuming and unpretending person to a degree remembered even to the present day. To give only one example: he had the key to a friend's house in Stockholm and was allowed to go in whenever he liked. Once he arrived late at night and did not wish to trouble the servants. So he slept in an office, on a wooden bench, with his great coat as a blanket. And that was in his last years of illness.

"His spontaneous goodness made him so considerate in all his dealings with people that he was reproached for not defending himself sufficiently, especially when anyone was insolent towards him personally. But he was not a coward. He did not feel uncomfortable when standing alone. In an important vote in his last conference of the Swedish bishops—it was on the Eisenach Resolution, which dealt with the possibility of a divergence between the attitudes of the church and of the state to a final appeal to a court of arbitration in the event of imminent war—he remained alone, in opposition to all his colleagues. But when delegates from the whole church met in a free conference he had the joy of persuading the lay bench and of gaining victory. From the oecumenical standpoint Professor Siegmund-Schultze testifies that 'He had a personal courage which I scarcely ever found in a church leader. He was deliberately incautious.'"

§

When he became sixty years old, the Stockholm free-church newspaper, comparing him with his predecessors, wrote, "Nathan Söderblom is at once a prelate, a brilliant researcher and a truly Christian man." And Bishop Ammundsen, a writer of church history, says that "he combined the three principal church types: the inwardness of revival, the taste for research, culture and social tasks found in liberalism, and the love of the typical churchman for old institutions which were to be filled with new content."

Of his alleged weakness for power and pomp I would say, he had them, though he had them not.

"He was not stubborn. He could adhere firmly to his opinion, but he could also give in all of a sudden and eagerly accept objections. I know by experience that he genuinely relished opposition. K. B. Westman, now professor at Uppsala, and I sat together as secretaries in the archbishop's study through the night during the church unity conference at Uppsala in 1917: we had to draft resolutions in accordance with what had been said in the conversations. We sat in our shirt-sleeves and each strove to word them carefully in the languages entrusted to us — German and English — while Söderblom paced up and down gesticulating and talking. He found astonishing formulas—he was a master of that—and we faithfully wrote them down, as though they were grains of gold. But sometimes we could not make something agree with what we had already written, or a phrase proved when more closely analysed to be ambiguous or tendencious. I do not know how many times—at first with shy anxiety—we said: 'No, archbishop, that won't do!' Hearing our reasons, he would laugh and say, 'No, certainly not!' and gladly begin afresh. Such manners are not those of a dictator. Once, when it was a question of the opportunities which power gives, he said that both these and their abuse could be abolished, but sin within us could not. But it is habit that first shows whether sin has been allowed to dominate us. With Söderblom, Christ's refining fire was too glowing for any secular desire for power to take root and become innate in him.

" 'Weakness for pomp?' Papers were full of pictures of him wearing vestments—'Those awful papers,' he would say—and so he had often to hear about 'romanizing tendencies' and 'church wardrobes.' But he only followed the established customs and usages of Swedish Lutheranism. What was new was that people looked to him who understood to give a new importance to what had always existed. He did not wish to introduce innovations in worship. Here, too, he felt the freedom and quietness of being allowed to tread in the footsteps of the fathers. It was dead routine that was removed, and thereby custom regained its genuine meaning and power. As a good Lutheran he saw that everything depended upon the spirit which was dominant. Puritanism, democratic nationalism, high-churchmanship—they were all equally likely to disclose something of the Evil One if they were allowed to become the main principle in a Christian's life. 'If something beside the Saviour himself and the love for truth comes to be the main factor in a church, that comes of evil.' Of the archiepiscopal cope he would say, 'Sometimes it requires courage to wear it'; but when he wore it, it bore him up, for it made him feel, as he said, 'a short link in a long chain.'

"The fact that the main point was to him the main point, and that a secondary matter was secondary, that his inward freedom depended on being centrally bound to the one thing needful, gave him complete outward freedom to move within any form of worship whatsoever. He was able to make significant whatever form of worship he used. Perhaps that was why he was thought to be dangerous. Or was it something else? Söderblom often made things preach sermons. When, during an act of consecration from the altar, he made his crozier resound on the paving, it was as if 'the long chain,' the linking of generations, underlined the words just spoken and gave them a new power. When, in his cope and with his crozier, he pointed at the pulpit or at the font in consecrating them, it was as if something came out of him. 'That is a dangerous fellow,' rustics would say. Vestments and ceremonies were for Söderbolm symbols of two things—of the continuity of the Church throughout the centuries, and of what is mysterious in the very idea of the house and minister of God, of what is incomprehensible in the meeting of a human soul with God himself.

"Moreover, Söderblom knew from the history of religion that religion is a drama, not obsolete views or passive contemplation, but activity, revelation, history, action—*drama*. The eye as well as the ear has its mission in the religious life: to let, by means of symbols, truth become the operative *power*. Thus the archbishop insisted firmly on the rich heritage of the Church handed down from the fathers in the realm of Sweden, and gave them a new impressiveness—which souls perceived, even if photographs toned it down.

"Was he high-church minded? If so, it is curious how he 'got away with' his complete openness towards low-churchmanship. When consecrating St. Ansgar's chapel in 1930, in the presence of the King of Sweden, the government, the aristocracy and the episcopate of the whole north, he thanked the chief of the Salvation Army for its collaboration, having managed to get its singers for the choral part of the service. He did not respect any man's person when the common Christian 'front' was at stake. He was not an 'oecumenical churchman' abroad and a high-churchman at home. So it was quite natural and, indeed, impressive at his funeral to see the chief representatives of the Swedish dissenting churches, with whom he had been associated at oecumenical conferences and whom he had always honoured, following as mourners behind the hearse of this 'prelate.' There was a universal oppenness in him and it was that which—both at home and abroad—made his surroundings so free and so sure. *Too* open, carelessly wide, as his adversaries in the bishopric of Göteborg never ceased to believe. But even the Eastern Orthodox and the Anglican Churches judged that Söderblom trod in the footsteps of the Shepherd of the sheep and saw his universalism to be Christ's own. And his good humour and his poetry were spread everywhere: 'It was like music around him and his path,' said the editor of *Socialdemokraten*.

"The humour of Söderblom was not Danish, with its play upon words, witticisms and anecdotes, or French, with its point, *esprit* and irony. It was rather Attic—salt and smile in one: but above all it was Northern, Swedish, revealing the leafy wood and the brook's ripples, a sympathetic nearness, containing merriment and poetry at the same time. Söderblom was full of song. In the middle of an address given at a banquet in America he did not mind singing a revivalist song, and in his last broadcast address about Luther, a hymn. Wherever he trod, his eyes were seeking out beauty, in art or in nature, as the bee seeks out the flower. One savours the honey in the whole of his speech. He could not refrain from visiting the lilies of the field.

"I have wandered a good deal from my point: Which was the greater, his genius or his character? But it is useful to let the single features speak for themselves. There may be many fragments of marble on the ground where such a statue was chiselled out—so let those who pass by collect what they may find. But as time passes Söderblom's inner attitude and achievement will entirely dominate the memory of him, and I think I may already dare to sum up.

"The peculiarity of Söderblom was seen in a harmony of powers and character, of gifts and a goal of cosmic inclusiveness. He has not produced works of special genius. When his discourses made such a deep impression, it was often because they formed the text upon which his soul's experience had built its orchestral unity of words, personality and work within himself. And we get nowhere if we try to isolate these elements one from another. His genius is not to be found in any one of the limited spheres within which he worked. But no talent worked in him in isolation. The collaboration of his gifts had a result so remarkable that rare words are needed to characterize it.

"One cannot call love a quality of genius, but if the genius is filled with love, then both become the more remarkable. Söderblom's capacity for prodigality in devoting himself to human beings, in believing in them, in appreciating them, sprang from his reverence for and delight in every human being because each was a 'soul.' Therefore each individual was taken in his own specific way, and from that there grew in Söderblom a knowledge of persons, a faithfulness in remembrance, a discerning insight into the centre of each single man. He was fully at everybody's disposal. He did not give himself in bits, scantily measured—in this too he resembled the sun. But he was also guided by the leading orchestral discipline in the whole which we called 'character.' Sometimes one would feel bewildered when confronted by him, just as one might at the rehearsal of an orchestra when everything was still in chaos and each instrument went its own way. But he held the magic baton, and when he raised it one heard the 'music of the spheres' and realized that one comprehended him fully. This realization always came when seeing him concerned with his life's work. For it is part of the secret of Söderblom that he was himself only when engaged in creative activity. His personality can never be distinguished from his activity, for the basic motive of his life was his desire to share by service in God's creative activity. In the last resort he saw himself simply as a tool at the Master's disposal. And here it happens that all gifts given to him by nature or grace come into a living unity. He is the peerless instrument with so rich an arrangement of stops that his Lord could produce from him such varied music as to make many hear each the special melody of his own calling. He was an organ blown by the winds of Heaven, and here—as a servant, as an instrument in the greatest work —his genius was finally and particularly to be found.

"So it is artificial to try to discriminate between his character and his genius. Without this character his genius would not have become creative; but, quite certainly, when isolated from the genius, the character would have been something different, resembling position without personality. But that they did find each other—Lo! this is the work of God, this is Nathan Söderblom."

2

I PASS on to three among eleven contributions constituting the remarkable work *Nathan Söderblom: In Memoriam*.

Professor Tor Andrae, now bishop of Linköping, author of the best biography of Söderblom, gives a careful estimate of him as a religious historian. To begin with he sets out the bewildering manysidedness of Söderblom's spiritual equipment and activity. Nevertheless, he says, there is a distinct main line of thought going through and characterizing Söderblom's theological output.

Söderblom was in the first place endeavouring to obtain a concrete conception of the history of religion and, secondly, to give a true interpretation of this history in order to show it as an irrefutable testimony to the incomparable greatness of the Christian faith, the unique character of which he had learnt to grasp through the inspiration of Ritschl and grappling with his thought. Söderblom truly represents that type of scholar whose primary gift is the faculty of entering into the object of his research, so that he is enabled to see with its eyes, to feel what it is feeling, and to think its thoughts, and this through a sense of solid reality and not through logic. And he always tried to avoid pressing comparisons too far.

This trait is connected with another emphasized by Andrae: Söderblom recognized that God and his word need no advocate, his soul's deliverance had been won. The secret of his "apologetics" was that a radiant certainty of the absolute superiority of genuine Lutheranism had released him, once and for all, from any anxiety. Thus he was set free for research, which became a means of showing the pre-eminence of the Christian faith in an evangelistic way. He was so free that, with a rare "generosity," as Andrae styles it, which might be misleading to outsiders, he came more and more, in the oecumenical discussion, to expend intense love and labour on those aspects of religion which were the more foreign to his own. So he entered deeper and deeper into the problems of mysticism.

But, as Andrae remarks, it is not likely that his increasing appreciation of mysticism, under the influence of Frederick von Hügel, Inge and the English platonists, culminating in his Gifford lectures of 1931, was caused by a corresponding religious development of his own. It is true that there were certain parallelisms, among others the ascetic training of the will, common to him and his father. "His sympathy with mysticism is very obvious where he speaks *about* religion. But one gets a different impression from his utterances *in* religion; his own teaching moves in the spiritual world of confidence and forgiveness. It has no mystical element. It was the endeavour of his comprehensive oecumenical spirit to understand this piety, which presented the spiritual life of Christianity with so many of its most remarkable figures, more deeply, that brought Söderblom nearer to mysticism. His faculty of understanding by means of religious psychology took a new and important step forward in the Gifford lectures, that last work which worthily crowns his theological life-work."

§

Professor Gustaf Aulén, now bishop of Strängnäs, examines the character of Söderblom's theological achievement.[1] He starts by observing how much, amid all the other tasks of his life, theological research work meant to Söderblom, and what extreme concentration and exertion of will had to be applied to enable him to make his way to a professorship in the midst of a laborious *diaspora* ministry

[1] A translation has been published in the *Church Quarterly Review*, vol. 115 (1932–3), pp. 15–48.

and, later on, to make feasible further research work in addition to the requirements of his widening and increasingly absorbing duties.

Emphasizing the main tendencies, Aulén shows what a great deliverance Ritschl effected for Söderblom, as well as how Söderblom's most characteristic achievements resulted in a breaking-up of the remaining narrownesses of Ritschlianism. Being a son of revival, Söderblom did not at all share Ritschl's cool objectiveness. Unfolding the historical character of the "continued revelation" (*Gifford Lectures*, x), he both draws from Ritschl and far out-does him. His differentiation between the religions which represent the mysticism of infinity and that of personal relation to God is not conceivable without Ritschl; his way of making concrete the "continued revelation," by showing that it takes place in church history, lies far beyond Ritschl's possibilities. Two aspects determine Söderblom's new avenues and offer a solid basis to his oecumenical activity: "One is his orientation towards the history of religions, setting him free from all sorts of doctrinaire assumptions about primitive Christianity and the true nature of the Christian faith itself. The other is the way in which he gives the central place to what I would call the classical and monumental features of the Christian faith. Söderblom's view combines these two factors—and this is rare. His importance as a theologian may be seen more in this combination than in anything else."

§

The contribution of Professor Yngve Brilioth, now bishop of Växiö, concerns us most. In its conciseness, its systematic sequence and pithy pregnancy he gives an entire history of the oecumenical movement such as we had not yet had, his emphasis always being laid on the history of Söderblom, the man, the specialist and the churchman. He can do so because Söderblom's life history was connected with oecumenical endeavours of which no branch remained foreign to him.

"The evangelical renewal of the Church was purchased at a high price: the shattering of the outward unity of the Western church. The history of the Church after the Reformation deals to a great extent with a continued scattering. Within Lutheran Christianity provincialism became prevalent. It is as if Luther had foreknown this danger when, in the introduction to his *Deutsche Messe*, he suggested that young people should be taught foreign languages so that, unlike the Waldensians in Bohemia, they should not 'imprison their faith within their own language' but be able to witness for it before men of other tongues. In the Lutheran Church the unity of the Church became an article of faith which had little relation to outward reality. The inter-church movement, in which Archbishop Söderblom stands out as playing the leading part, means, from one aspect, a breaking-down of the provincialness of Lutheranism. At the same time and above all it means that the doctrine of the unity of the Church has been rediscovered as a matter essential for Christian faith. For those who have made this discovery, work for the outward realization of church unity is not only a matter of practical convenience, but an imperative obligation. The archbishop's outward activity was closely connected with his inward development on this point. There was an unbroken connection between them during his whole life.

"In the history of the Church of Sweden it was perhaps the nineteenth century which saw the culmination of provincialism with regard to good churchmanship and orthodox theology. Only one view was left—

towards the chairs of the German 'fathers of the Church.' Even to her Northern neighbour churches the door was opened only occasionally and half-way. English-speaking Christendom was 'the origin and source of all sectarianism.' When the evangelical alliance, in the footsteps of the great popular revival, tried to unite devout souls above creed and nationality, its individualism excited opposition among church people. The Church of England was, in the main, an unknown world. It will scarcely be an anticipation of the judgement of history if we characterize the breaking-down of provincial narrowness, above all during the second and third decade of the twentieth century, as the preliminary steps to a new epoch in the life of our church.

"What happened here has certainly not been only one man's work. But, as usually happens at turning-points in history, the call, the task at hand, produced its man, one with a specially suitable equipment, who did not hesitate to go forward once the inner urgency was perceived, and who later on was led to a greater achievement than he or others foresaw.

"Two factors, closely related to one another, trained and prepared Nathan Söderblom for his oecumenical task: the interest in missionary work in his parental home, and the Student Christian Movement. His theological development laid the foundation of a theological oecumenicity which, never being strictly severed from the ecclesiastical, presupposed it. With the gradual widening of his spiritual horizon the specific and valuable peculiarity of his Lutheran inheritance was put in a new and clearer light. There is a deep continuity to be observed between the first theological essays of the student and his completed work.

"The years passed in Paris proved to be of fundamental importance for his theological oecumenicity.

It is to be emphasized that they gave him the international orientation, the European frame of mind, which distinguished him from almost all contemporary Swedish theologians. They were balanced and complemented by his years spent as a professor at Leipzig. Here he achieved a personal union with German theology and church-life which made the world war an intensely personal problem for him. Without the authority and the confidence acquired during the years passed in Germany, strengthened and deepened by his charitable activity in the later years of the war, he would not have been able to act as a bridge-builder between English and German Christianity.

"At home also theological oecumenicity paved the way for ecclesiastical. At a time when a sense of the dominant position of German theology paralysed all confidence in the possibilities of Swedish, it gave an impression of boldness, and at the same time a sense of relief, when the man who knew best the real importance of German theology could venture to put forward the idea that one day a German might find it worth while to study theology in Sweden. The formation of the Olaus Petri foundation in 1908, which to a certain degree may have depended upon Söderblom's initiative, essentially contributed to a widening of the Swedish theological horizon, above all by the chance it gave to hear foreign lecturers. Allowances from its funds enabled a number of young theologians to become familiar with new worlds.

"Mainly through Söderblom's endeavours during his Uppsala professorship, a door which had been closed for centuries came to be re-opened. When the connection between the Churches of England and Sweden was remade, memories of the time of the conversion of Sweden were revived, and a foundation was laid for later oecumenical work which must not be underrated. Söderblom stirred up in individual students the idea, odd and almost heretical from the point of view of older Swedish university theology, that even in England there could be something for a theologian to learn, and not least within the Church of England. Above all, it was due to him that the opportunity of approach between the churches was seized and utilized. At the Lambeth Conferences of 1888 and 1897 attention had been drawn to the Church of Sweden which, by its unbroken apostolic succession, seemed to offer possibilities for a closer connection. But the interest remained for a long time academic.

"Before the Lambeth Conference of 1908 a new venture of approach was made from the English side. Through the Swedish legation in London a proposal was sent to Archbishop Ekman to examine the possibilities of a closer connection between the two churches. It was the eager interest taken by Professor Söderblom in the matter, when he saw the letter during an interview with the archbishop, which caused negotiations to be commenced and, mainly through him, continued. He even participated in a congress at Oxford in the same year, and on this journey made acquaintance with English churchmen.

"It was only fourteen years later that he saw the happy issue of the negotiations between the two churches, which he had also furthered by publications. Already before their beginning, in 1909, he sketched with rare clear-sightedness the historical peculiarity of the Church of England and its conditions for a further connection which should not obliterate the lines of demarcation. The idea of Christian unity as a basic motive is emphatically maintained: 'Here, without glossing over confusion and inconsiderate zeal, with clear and quiet insight into that which unites and that which separates, at a precise point, an expressive demonstration can be found for the unity of Christendom between two churches, both too zealous in truthfulness and faithfulness to themselves to initiate intimate intercourse on superficial and half-true grounds.' But his reports suffer from a serious incompleteness: they pass over in silence his own inspiring contribution."

After having given a short sketch of the negotiations, and having paid due homage to Bishop John Wordsworth, Brilioth goes on:

"What was reached was more than a formal agreement. The convergence of the Churches of England and Sweden has become a reality to a much greater extent than the members of the conference of 1909 could have expected. A new bearing had been taken, not least in Swedish church life, and perhaps that will come to stand out one day as marking two periods in the history of our church. Of course this corresponds to the cultural reorientation after the war which turned the face of Sweden more to the west. But the contact between the churches was begun earlier, and the roads which it paved have proved to be of the greatest importance for the new orientation of the spiritual life connected with the new cultural bearing. Its results have as yet become only partly obvious, but a factor has been introduced into our spiritual life which was not there before. What has happened here ought not to be forgotten when one speaks of the oecumenical work of Nathan Söderblom.

"The English relations had direct reactions even on himself and contributed to prepare the ground for future work. The circle of his personal acquaintances was widened, and came finally to include most of the leaders of the Church of England.

"There is no doubt that England and its national church were of great importance to him personally. Connections with it strengthened the oecumenical turn of his mind—here the 'walls' became 'transparent' in a special sense. The Church of England captured him by the power of her devotional life and her endeavour to serve. Certainly in this way his own appreciation of the historical continuity of the Church of Sweden, of her suggestive historical ceremonies and of her deep Catholicism, came to be even more developed. But for the legalistic, one-sidedly romanizing ritualism of some Anglo-Catholics he had no sympathy—though he knew with a remarkable freedom from bias, here as everywhere, how to value the reality of a religious life even where it assumed expressions which gave him little pleasure. He himself used liturgical ceremonies with the independent freedom of the heir who is of age and feels responsibility. He perceived at an early stage of his career the comprehensiveness which characterizes the life of the Church of England, and he has often emphasized it. He may have valued highest the broad-church element, but he was certainly greatly impressed by the noble high-church piety of the older type as represented by the aged Bishop Talbot, and by the younger liberally-inclined wing of this element, especially since it took over from the broad-church its heritage of social endeavour—here our thought goes first to Archbishop William Temple. But he always realized that the connection with England should never be allowed to affect the close affinity of the Church of Sweden with her Lutheran sister churches and with Protestant Christianity as a whole. The new perspective for his church was valuable to him mainly because it set that church the honourable task of uniting the principal sections of Evangelical Christianity. Thus his connection with Anglicanism contributed to his personal preparation for his great task.

"The Anglican connections are paralleled, or rather balanced, by his period as professor in Leipzig, 1912–1914. There were no negotiations of ecclesiastical policy required to open the way to the Lutheran churches of Germany: this way always stood open. So the rich and in many respects happy years at Leipzig were of great importance for his oecumenical work. In this connection it is not irrelevant to remark that the time of Söderblom's perfect scientific maturity, which is marked by his book on *The Origin of Belief in God*, was passed in the intimate intercourse of research with German theology before its flourishing state was over. By this the foundation was laid for the confidence, scarcely exceeded for any other neutral personage in a responsible position, shown in him by the German side during the years of disaster. It was also fortunate that his familiarity with German spiritual life attained its perfection in Lutheran surroundings. He entered a faculty of Lutherans at a high stage of development; among colleagues such as R. Kittel, the elder Althaus, Ihmels, Hauck and Rendtorff his awareness of the indispensable importance of Lutheran theological tradition was confirmed—a value which a single body ought not to preserve for itself alone, but should make accessible to others. During later years his endeavours for church unity sometimes met with distrust on the part of Lutherans of the stricter and narrower observance; and it was a great advantage to him that, when he thus faced guardians of the creed who adhered to its letter, he could, as a real Lutheran theologian, point out the living personal source of this creed. The younger

Lutheranism, deepened by research, must see in him its captain in face of a confessionalism which, in far too high a degree, has assumed the control of Lutheran collaboration. Söderblom's familiarity with Luther, begun in the years of his youth, was developed and strengthened during the time in Leipzig, which also gave him an opportunity of repeated visits to the historical places of the Reformation. It bore its most mature fruit much later in his book on Luther, *Humour and Melancholy*, a book which is something of a personal confession and at the same time an historical description, a testimony to a deep congeniality between author and subject. For him Lutheranism and oecumenical comprehensiveness are not opposed: they condition and support each other.

"Not least important were Söderblom's experiences at the outbreak of the war of 1914-18. He was then in Germany, and there followed a troublesome journey back to his native country. To his immediate impressions of the national enthusiasm of the time, which he kept in living remembrance and to which he often reverted in discourse and writing, there was added the thought of his personal friends on the other side, of the portentous significance of the catastrophe both for mankind and for Christendom. For a man so intimately connected with all that was most noble in the world of men and thought, neutrality did not mean a cool self-sufficient looking-on, but an intense fellow suffering, closely connected with a theologian's deepened penetration into the mystery of the Cross. At the beginning of 1915 Professor A. Deissmann wrote, with the clear-sightedness of a friend, about Söderblom's reaction to the war: 'When I reflect upon the way in which this whole war affects him, whom I know personally and admire highly, I find only one word to express the holy sufferings in the depths of his Christian soul: Yea, a sword shall pierce through thine own soul also.'"

§

Having now been brought by Brilioth to the threshold of the war, we can no longer follow his thorough account describing Söderblom's oecumenical efforts during that time, from Oud Wassenaer to Stockholm, the Stockholm and Lausanne Conferences, and those of the following years. We must confine ourselves to the most important and characteristic points. Brilioth mentions the formation of the World Alliance for Promoting International Friendship through the Churches, at Constance on the memorable August 2, 1914, and gives the history of the whole series of appeals "for peace and Christian fellowship" emanating from Uppsala and promulgated by the united northern primates; the first of them was signed even by a few church leaders from belligerent countries.

"The circle of subscribers had dwindled away since 1914, yet now came a rather unexpected echo. At the annual meeting of the British Friends in May 1917, a resolution was proposed in which the Christians of all nations were admonished to unite in prayer 'for forgiveness, for light, for reconciliation.' Thence also arose the idea of an international meeting. The initiative of the Friends led to the formation of the British Council for Promoting an International Christian Meeting. At this point the British and Swedish endeavours met. The British committee itself exhorted the subscribers of the neutral appeal to address themselves to a wider circle, including the Roman Catholic and Eastern Orthodox Churches.

"Knowledge of the existence of the British council and its activity was a powerful and encouraging incentive for the archbishop. There was another. At this time there appeared an English weekly, *The Challenge*, which with dauntless ardour pleaded for the social duties of the church. Its editor was the Reverend William Temple (later Archbishop of Canterbury). In September 1917 he expressed in an editorial his deep regret that the international workmen's conference proposed during the war—oddly enough at Stockholm—was to be concelled: now, he said, it was the duty of the Church to try to bring about 'an international interdenominational conference.' When Archbishop Söderblom read the articles in *The Challenge* he was deeply moved—what he read there tallied with the feeling of his inmost heart; here the thought with which he had wrestled was openly set forth. He expressed this in his own contribution to *The Challenge* of November 23. From these English exhortations he gained an incentive to enlarge the intended meeting of representatives of the World Alliance and to have a universal church conference. The conference of December 1917 was attended only by neutrals, chiefly Scandinavians.

"A preliminary sketch for the programme of the future world conference contained three points: 1. The Unity of Christians, 2. Christians and the Common Life, 3. Christians and Law and Order. Here it was obvious that a deeper penetration into the problem of Christian unity must lead to dealing with the class and racial problems which later on were the centre of the programme of the Stockholm Conference. But the far-sighted and strongly religious formulation of the idea of unity is also important: 'This unity which is centred in the cross of Christ ought to be brought nearer to reality in life and teaching than hitherto—without being ungrateful for or faithless to the special gifts of Christian experience and insight which each church body has received from the God of history'.

"The archbishop never saw his eagerly planned conference gather in 1918. Both he and the enterprise were matured through this failure. Step by step he had gained approbation for his projects. Even when people were inclined to consider the whole thing with patronizing superiority, they felt compelled to respect a will which no setbacks could shake. The signals from Uppsala had told of a given meeting-place, they had given a common bearing to the thoughts and hopes of many, not least in the belligerent countries. For himself, he had learnt many things, and especially had his understanding of the leading personalities become more exact. Thus his own plans gained in power and inward stability, and to this the series of Olaus Petri lectures devoted to the problem of church unity also contributed. They are one of the most important monuments in the history of the oecumenical movement.

"For analysing the development of the archbishop's oecumenical thought, we have to break off in 1918, at a decisive year. In his essay on 'Evangelical Catholicism' he writes on the most straightforward lines, and theological motives are given for his 'oecumenical system' which recur later in different variations and are further unfolded in his later works. The theology of the Cross becomes the centre even of his oecumenical thinking. The rescuing of culture depends upon the salvation of individuals: 'The old man in ourselves, represented by denominational narrowness and ignorance, and by conceited disdain of other communities, must be smothered and killed, and the love of Christ must increase in us day by day. The Saviour embraces Christianity with his arms outstretched on the cross.' At Oud Wassenaer in 1919 Söderblom's leadership in oecumenical work began in earnest."

As the influence of Archbishop Johansson of Åbo continued to be a main source of the opposition which unceasingly met Söderblom's oecumenical endeavours in wide Lutheran circles, both at home and abroad, Brilioth's description of its reasons deserve attention, the more because he had the opportunity of making a close study of Johansson while he was a professor in Åbo.

"Besides a general mistrust of the so-called 'modern theologians' who collaborated at Stockholm, or announced their approval of the conference, he was influenced by the theological principles received from the teacher of his early years, J. T. Beck. Johansson stood out as the last champion of Beck's one-sidedly eschatological interpretation of Christianity. According to this view, the Church has no other aim than to save individual souls whilst expecting the final judgement; and, in face of an enterprise like the Stockholm Conference which endeavoured to make Christianity and the Church factors in social and economic life, he felt bound, with Beck, to consider it, literally and sincerely, to be a work of Antichrist. In his book about the Stockholm Conference Söderblom expresses his appreciation of the consistency characterizing the actions and words of his brother dignitary, paralleling Johansson's opposition to the conference with his not yielding on matters of principle to the Russian government during the years of the Finnish disaster in the beginning of this century.

"In this connection I may recall the last meeting of the two archbishops, two years after the Stockholm Conference. The symbolic importance of the conference gave to their meeting an interest for church history. Here, in peculiarly typical staunch representatives, two epochs, to a certain extent two types of

Christianity, faced one another. Being the only witness of their conversation, I may be excused for giving some recollections of it.

"It was on October 3, 1927, when Archbishop Söderblom during a stay in Åbo visited the archbishop's house. The Archbishop of Finland met him with impulsive vivacity, and pronounced his lively displeasure with what was said of him in Söderblom's book on the Stockholm Conference ('This book I can't approve of'), with its attempts to induce the Church to interfere in the things of this world ('This is childish'—he repeated with great eagerness), and its connection with Harnack and other dangerous theologians. When Söderblom tried to give a biblical foundation for his work, taken from the Prophets and the Gospels, he was met by the insistence that no biblical support whatever could be found for the ideas of the Stockholm Conference: it was not concerned with penitence and conversion. I almost expected an anathema to conclude the conversation; but the subject was changed. Then, away from the sphere of controversy, Johansson was brought to speak about his recollections of the Finnish Revival, in which he had shared in his youth; the old man thawed, and his natural cordiality broke through. He spoke with warmth of church people he had met on his visitations—but at the same time he felt bound to add that they were quite untouched by the ideas of Stockholm! The conversation ended in a friendly way. The old archbishop was pleased at an invitation to celebrate the memory of Gustavus Adolphus on November 6 in Uppsala, which, however, considerations of health compelled him to decline.

"While extreme Lutheranism remained aloof, the leading men of the Lutheran Church of Germany had definitely espoused the cause of the conference. That Landesbischof Ihmels of Saxony pleaded with power and clearness for German Lutheranism at Stockholm, and afterwards faithfully collaborated in the work of the continuation committee, is a fact the importance of which becomes clearest against the actual background of the declining position of Lutheran sectarianism. This meant that conscious German Lutherans in 'Life and Work' found a suitable form of participation in church-unity activity, which opened up a way for new collaboration between them and English churchmen, even in questions which, strictly judged, lie beyond the programme of Stockholm. It is not easy to decide with certainty how much the influence of Söderblom helped to make this possible. But it is certain that no contemporary churchman could fill his place in this precise respect."

The bold adventure of the Stockholm Conference and the urgent need which the archbishop often felt to make decisions personally without consulting his colleagues were justified by the result of the conference. Brilioth is right in saying:

"Looking back on the decisive points of his life, one involuntarily recollects his words to his surgeon when he awoke from the anaesthetic after his operation on July 10, 1931: 'The most important thing in life is to take responsibility.' The divergence between him and the international committee was due essentially to his demand for a programme prearranged to the last detail. The issue is the best proof that he was right. The high standard maintained by most of the chief addresses at the conference would scarcely have been reached without his insistence on defining promptly the task of each speaker. He took quite special pains to ensure that the different communities and peoples should all be allowed to speak in proper rotation, and that no church body, especially the smaller, should feel forgotten. In this he was helped by his incomparable knowledge of people.

"It remains briefly, and without claiming completeness, to indicate how some other lines were continued until the end. One of these is northern collaboration. The conferences of northern bishops went smoothly. The last followed the consecration of St. Ansgar's chapel on Björkö, at which northern guests participated as well as representatives of the different free churches of Sweden. Björkö chapel, to which the archbishop gave so much loving thought, also in a measure stands as a monument to his oecumenical work, and to the convergent aims of his life work also. In the same summer of 1930 he was able to participate in the anniversary of St. Olav at Trondhjem and Stiklastad, and there to see 'a people on the mountain of transfiguration'—and to bear witness to his vision in words which became treasured by the Christians of Norway.

"It is in connection with northern collaboration that his work for Lutheran unity is to be considered. We have to remember that this is not covered by the movement which found its expression in the Lutheran World Convention. The archbishop was not in very close contact with the convention, but this was not because he lacked interest in the idea of uniting Lutheran churches —he saw in it a necessary link in endeavours for church unity. This came to light on different occasions, chiefly at Lausanne. He participated actively in the Lutheran World Convention at Copenhagen in spite of great bodily weakness. All his unsparing self-command was required for seeing through what he had undertaken—

a lecture in Copenhagen cathedral and a speech at the dedication of the Knights' Hall at Kronborg castle. But his freer and more spiritual understanding of the basic ideas of the creed and his wider perspective in ecclesiastical politics seem to have been considered with a certain mistrust by the leaders of the convention. Thus the Lutheran unity movement lost the spiritual asset of his personal influence, and it even came to lose contact with the younger generation of scientifically-trained Lutheran theologians. It did not even succeed in becoming organically connected with the chief worldwide unity movements. But it was first of all due to Söderblom that, nevertheless, the leading Lutheran churches of Europe became actively engaged in the oecumenical movement characterized by the name 'Stockholm.' And it is surely no exaggeration to say that no contemporary has done more for making Luther's thought heard within non-Roman Western Christianity.

"About the achievement of the archbishop in the life of the universal Church, the Bishop of Chichester writes that he personally could 'have no doubt that Archbishop Söderblom did more than any other church leader of his day, by direct work and by his enthusiastic and resolute persuasion of others in many lands, to draw, or rather to begin the drawing, together of the churches of all nations in Christian service and Christian work (*Communio Oecumenica in serviendo*).'

"When he reached the end of his road, the personal authority he had acquired without aspiring after it had become a uniting factor in Christendom. His great importance in this respect can be revealed gradually by seeing how he left the different forms of the Church Militant. He did not leave a completed task, but a work which was still in full progress: at his empty place the tools lie ready, as they fell from his hand. For those who had collaborated with him, especially in oecumenical work, he therefore remains a companion and an inspiration. In his last spring he gave the Gifford lectures, on 'The Living God,' at Edinburgh. With heartfelt joy was he able to resume oecumenical work in the realm of research, which had preceded his oecumenical church work. It was interrupted, but it makes his life better remembered in this respect. On the way home he discussed with his old friend Bishop Hensley Henson in Durham the question of parliamentary interference, which was then a burning one in the Church of England. Once more, as Lord Parmoor's guest, he was comforted by the quietness of the English countryside. His last day of good health he spent in visiting the English-Scandinavian theological conference on Sparreholm. Some of its members were staying in his house during his illness and were the object of his solicitude until the last, and in order to carry out his prearranged plans they undertook a pilgrimage to St. Ansgar's chapel in Björkö the day after his death.

"The Church of Sweden was not only brought out of its provincial isolation by Söderblom, it was given a leading position within Christendom. By virtue of this one man's spiritual achievement it seemed to have recovered the international significance it had once before possessed (though then it had not been of the same extent) in virtue of the political position of the kingdom. Certainly it cannot maintain this position, since the personal support which made it possible no longer exists; but what has happened is neither a mere episode nor a dream. For the Church of Sweden, as well as for the universal Church, something has happened which cannot be undone, bonds have been tied which cannot again be severed, perspectives have been opened which cannot again be veiled, our church has been set in a connection from which it cannot be torn away. Oecumenical action has become a factor in its development, a task which must not be betrayed."

3

SÖDERBLOM's work for reunion is only properly to be understood if we realize that it was bound up with the yet more practical problems of social and international reconstruction. Bishop Ammundsen's analysis is perhaps the most clear: "If the Church is to serve the present, it must bear this generation's burdens. It must strike an intellectual balance and must understand the social need. If the Church is to serve, it must be reawakened and must overcome its pettiness and divisions, which are an offence against the suffering world. And there is no better means of uniting those who are divided in matters of faith and order than coming to grips with this need and feeling our responsibility and our guilt. If one understands this connection, the interrelation between reunion and 'Life and Work' can no longer be ignored." In the words of the Bishop of Chichester, spoken at the tenth anniversary of Söderblom's death: "Many men at different times have worked and prayed for the reunion of Christendom. What, I think, was the new factor introduced by Söderblom was the vivid way in which his passion for Christian unity joined in with his passion for peace and for social justice. It is, I think, pretty clear that his method of achieving Christian unity, the method of love, as opposed to the Roman method of absorption and the Wittenberg method of faith, besides avoiding all problems of a purely ecclesiastical kind, offers a motive for Christian unity which is higher than any other motive, and has the capacity for marshalling all Christian forces, irrespective of denomination, as one body crusading against the cruelties and corruptions, the hatreds and wars of the world."

§

There are two distinct problems, that of social justice within each nation and that of relations between nations, based upon distinctly Christian standards. I proceed from the narrower to the wider problem.

A social hero is born, not made. This was certainly the case with Söderblom. He grew up in a country vicarage, where his father, being of yeoman stock, managed the glebe-land himself and imposed on his sons a great deal of hard work from their early years onward. When still a student with brilliant prospects, the eldest, Nathan, knew beforehand that there would not be much time for his studies during the holidays he spent at home. His father was an ascetic, denying any comfort to himself and to his children. A chair with a back, presented by a friendly churchwarden to the boys' household in the town where they went to school, had to be given back, the father allowing nothing but a three-legged stool, to prevent "effeminacy." And the elder Söderblom was zealous in striving to save souls: the children never forgot their dismay when at home one evening they found an old drunkard among those assembled for evening prayers. Instead of the dreadful things they expected to happen, he proved to have been converted and meekly joined in the prayers and hymns. Far from having an atmosphere likely to foment social prejudice, such a home produced a lasting experience of that which all human beings have in common as children of God.

This taught an unforgettable lesson to the student, the pastor, the professor, and the archbishop. Bishop Andrae observes: "When listening to Nathan Söderblom speaking to country folk during his visitations, one had to marvel at his complete naturalness and lack of affectation. The fact that he knew from practical experience the significance of really hard manual labour helped greatly to give him a sound sense of reality and insight into the condition of manual workers and their ways of thinking. He knew how the man behind the plow and on the cart looks at the world." He knew the right word and deed to comfort them in their distress, and all his wide interests were concentrated on the task of solving their problems along the lines of the Gospel. In this descendant of Swedish yeomen and Danish professional men no subsequent learning succeeded in warping his straightforward nature: this was instantly realized by his listeners, and thus he reached those who are generally out of range of the professional speaker. He won them by his sympathetic approach.

His joyfulness, purity and understanding were felt and remembered in later years equally clearly by the servants and labourers in whose work he had shared in his paternal home, by his school-fellows and by his university friends. One of his father's farm-labourers said that, "When working with me in the fields, he used to make up and sing verses about me and my horse." A Swedish vicar recollects seeing in the joiner's workshop connected with Uppsala University a fair-haired energetic person, at least a journeyman, as he thought, with admiration for his steady hand. Yet the man at the carpenter's bench proved to be "a student of five years' standing and consequently a graduate." "And so helpful and communicative he was, ready to become a freshman's friend and brother on the spot. To me our manual work signified the break through of democracy. The ideal was to be student as well as workman. My friend in his working-clothes, covered with the dust of the workshop, was a good comrade who cared for an unknown and lonely companion. I remember not a word of what he said—but he cared for us, his fellow workers. Later on he became an archbishop, and was still the same."

This rare openness to his neighbour, expressing a fervent endeavour to render to him the service which Christians owe to one another and, in their inmost heart, expect from one another, is seen in all the various phases of Söderblom's career.

"When in 1894 he had become chaplain to the Swedish legation in Paris, the special appropriateness of his gifts came to light. Here he had to minister to the Swedes and Norwegians in the capital, who formed a most variegated congregation, and even the Danes and Finns made him theirs. There were, besides the diplomats and other well-to-do people, many ordinary folk, and in addition a good deal of human wreckage of all sorts. He was expected to be the centre of attraction to gather these dispersed particles into a living unity. A great part of his activity consisted in meeting the crying needs of parishioners who were only loosely connected with the parish.

"It was this social activity that made him indispensable. He was the congregation's professional beggar, and he was understood and loved by his congregation. 'We were all human beings, and that was infinitely instructive. In this way also the power of Christ's gospel was put to the test.'

"Most instructive to him was the colony of Scandinavian artists. And exacting they were. He understood them and helped them, and they found their way back to their spiritual home, the church of their homeland. There was much poverty among them. 'For the time being I have been obliged to beg money for Strindberg, whose second wife has just left him and who is sick and wishes to go into hospital, and for a first-class Swedish sculptor.' Söderblom never met Strindberg personally, and took care that he never knew about the help extended to him. He thus avoided the indignation which the great misanthrope used to show towards any whom he knew to have put him under an obligation. He provided his artist friends with orders and gave them useful suggestions. When weak characters required a firm guidance to steel their wills and give buoyancy to their work, he would even take them into his home for months. So it is no wonder that, in an altar-piece in Calais chapel representing the Sermon on the Mount, one of the figures, a listening priest, bears Nathan Söderblom's features.

"There were some whose distress derived from other than economic sources. They did not fit conventional standards, and yet would look forward to the spell of understanding love which would set free what was best, yet deeply hidden, in the depths of their natures. Söderblom's letters particularly often mention Alfred Nobel, the inventor of dynamite and founder of the famous prize. It was the *man* that roused his interest. After his passing, Söderblom wrote to a friend: 'He was one of the most remarkable persons I ever met, a genius of creative power in the handling of matter. That which interested me most in him was his deep piety and his mistrust of all desire for wordly power asserting itself in the name of religion and the Church. He was considered anticlerical and an atheist. I came in touch with him in a peculiar way and gained his confidence. Then I came to see that, behind the old hermit's sceptical and negative modes of expression, and the desire for independence which was the result of his mistrust of his fellows, there was the soul of a child who hungered for and lived on love.' "

Bishop Andrae comments on this quotation by pointing to Söderblom's marvellous gift of detecting veins of precious metal where others saw only rugged mountain.

§

When he first entered on his duties in France it was summer, and he had to minister to the Swedish seamen at Calais.

"There the little chapel stood opposite to a seamen's inn, with which it was meant to compete; and on the top floor, next to the verger's quarters, there was a small attic with skylight, like a cabin, which was the chaplain's abode. During the day they, he and his young wife, his invaluable companion and helper who shared all his interests, kept to the reading-room, he with his book, she with her needlework. This gave the seamen a sense of homeliness and family life.

"The task of a chaplain to seamen requires a special vocational equipment, which Söderblom possessed. He had the courage to intrude when his ministry required it, and a special ability to strike the right note and to find points of contact with each individual. His sense of duty never allowed him to think of his own comfort. He had also, what was most important of all, a natural delicacy of feeling towards all who were neglected, which made of duty a joy. So he walked about the streets of the harbour district and the decks and cabins of the ships, cheerfully and dauntlessly inviting the sailors to the reading-room and the services. 'The religious tracts which people put into seamen's hands so often violate the principle that confidence is the only way to confidence. Devout zealots far too often believe in the magic effect of a few sheets of paper if only the names of God and Jesus and some biblical phrases are found on them.' He wanted to meet his seamen as a man among men, bringing a greeting from the homeland and the church where their souls were rooted. 'The best tract and invitation is the priest himself,' he used to say.

"In the summer of 1898 there were very few Swedish vessels in Calais: it seemed as though he would have a holiday, which would have been most welcome, as just then he was dealing with a great scholarly work. But Nathan Söderblom did not look at the matter in that way. A Swedish wholesale timber-merchant had fitted up a saw-mill in Coulogne, near Calais, and taken there about thirty Swedish workmen. Söderblom made up his mind to settle among them with his wife and three little ones, and hired a cottage, consisting of one room and a kitchen, with a floor of stamped earth, which was out of repair and primitive beyond description. He enjoyed this voluntary simplicity, while the workmen from the saw-mill felt at home in it. At the end of their day they flocked in and sat in the little kitchen. Nathan entertained them, and Anna gave them free lessons in French.

"In such surroundings Söderblom wrote his book on *The Sermon on the Mount and our Time*. This temporary return to conditions of primitive country life undoubtedly harmonized with his frame of mind and taste and roused recollections of the vicarage homes of his youth; but it was not indeed unconnected with the study of Tolstoy which just then occupied him intensely. Of course he was far from approving everything in the revolutionary ideas of the Russian prophet, yet for Söderblom he became a voice in the wilderness, the disturbing and uneasy conscience of the self-satisfied cultural religiosity of the end of the century. Under the influence of Tolstoy's revivalist teaching he saw Christianity and its founder in a new light. 'The real Jesus looks dangerous and revolutionary: dangerous for the self-satisfied quietness which praises its own virtues

—or bewails its own sins; revolutionary for the powers that hold us fast, or draw us back into indifference and fruitless complacency. Jesus was out of place in the community of his time and had to be made away with. And there was no proper place for the disciples who followed in his footsteps.' In the spiritual development of mankind Jesus is an eternal reproach and therefore an eternal stimulus.

"Among all the noises of the busy Paris capital one especially made itself felt to his sensitive mind, the rumbling subterranean roll which predicted outbursts and catastrophes, making itself heard out of the lower social strata upon which the brilliant cultural life of Paris is built. One of his first letters speaks of social unrest and the progress of anarchy. He felt his good fortune in belonging to 'the freest of all nations,' and only wished that his compatriots might understand the mission which at such a time was bound to be theirs.

"When still a student he had shown his interest in the social question, but it was in Paris that the problem forced itself upon him. He was stirred to the depths of his soul with indignation at the intolerable conditions under which Swedish seamen did their hard and badly-paid work. He had to watch a steamer leave for sea after being loaded as quickly as possible just on Christmas eve, so that it was only with great difficulty that he got the opportunity for a little improvised celebration at the last moment, to give the crew some reminder of the solemnity and joy of Christmas. Another steamer was to be loaded on Christmas day, and only the point-blank refusal of the French dock labourers saved the seamen their holiday. Söderblom's activity among the many poor in his Paris congregation gave him a clearer view of the needs of society.

"The feeling that Christianity and the Church did not

duly visualize their responsibility in view of the situation created by the new industrialism made him study the Christian social movement, as led by F. Naumann in Germany. He was deeply impressed by his experiences at the Evangelical Social Congress at Erfurt in November 1896, and by its brilliant and sturdy leader. '*Why* should the socialists always be the first to feel sympathy with those who come off worst in society and to condemn injustices?'

"This question may seem *naïf* for social thinking in terms of reality; yet it contains his social programme, the principle which governed his whole struggle for justice and social peace. So far from denying the necessity for the struggle of the working class, he pleaded with great determination for the freedom of the workers to form trades-unions: yet as a Christian he placed himself outside the struggle. He dared to believe that truth and justice and the restless pricking of the conscience are powers which can achieve something even within that objective order called the machinery of society. This *naïf* conviction of his is akin to that of the Sermon on the Mount and of St. Francis.

"In the spring of 1897 Söderblom studied the social question zealously. At the first Congress for the History of Religion, at Stockholm in the August of the same year, he gave an important lecture on *Religion and Social Development,* which a year later was published in German in an expanded form. He emphasizes that religion and society are two autonomous worlds, each following its own law, two spheres of life within both of which we can and ought to have rights of citizenship. They are linked together, and neither can exist without the other. Yet religion as such stands apart from and above society: Christ's kingdom is not of this world. From this it follows that the cause of religion never must be bound up with that of any political party, class or social programme. Religion exists for all.

"He feels a warm sympathy for the workmen's struggle for freedom and defends their cause boldly. They are grown men and do not want to be treated like children. They must be allowed to take their cause into their own hands, and their freedom of association and self-government must be recognized without haggling. As things are, the Christian ideal of love can and must take shape in certain definite demands; and the Church must herself plead for the workmen's right to work and for wages sufficient to secure an existence worthy of a human being, for adequate holidays and for the possibility of real home-life. Christianity ought to show its power and competence in that regard by deed and not by argument.

"In all essential points Söderblom faithfully adhered to this Christian social programme of his. The Church is to be the conscience of all parties and the property of the whole people. During his visitations Söderblom tried in this spirit to grapple with existing abuses and sometimes succeeded in bringing about an improvement, but perhaps more often gave offence to those who felt they had been interfered with.

"Söderblom used all his energy and brilliant eloquence to emphasize the position of the Church as a free spiritual body by the side of the state. It is easier to make such claims than to get them recognized and acted upon. Yet opponents, as well as pessimists within his own ranks, were bound to acknowledge that he did all a human will could to fulfil in the given circumstances the social duty of the Church. The greatest joy for him personally was that in the end he seemed to have succeeded in convincing even the Swedish workers that he wished them well with all his heart. Round his coffin there stood a people for once united in their sorrow.

"From the Congress for the History of Religion, and still occupied by serious social problems, he came to the brilliant festival with which Swedish students celebrated the twenty-five years' jubilee of King Oscar II. Part of it was an evening meeting in Uppsala botanical garden. There Söderblom happened on a workman busy with the lights which illuminated the wall of the building. The shadow of the man with bent back moved wearily and slowly across the bright wall, fantastically enlarged. From the garden could be heard the festive noise of the crowd around the loaded tables. Did nobody see the gigantic shadow on the wall?

"Stirred by this vision, Söderblom next day made an address which was quite outside the programme when he pleaded for the workers over against the privileged professional classes. 'Swedish students!' he exclaimed, 'Did you see him? Yesterday he revealed himself to me, as we always see him at a distance, shapeless, half without outline, enlarged like a spectre. Comrades, we do not know him! Yet now and then, at leisure and at work, we become aware of him, there remains an uncomfortable feeling which we would like to push away, especially from this our festive meeting. Did you see him?' He spoke of the shadow on the wall, of the worker with his heavy toil and straitened conditions. 'What did he think when he saw the hosts of happy young people, the Sunday's-children of our nation, during a brilliant festival week like this? We must get to know him, not by deliberate fraternization, but by acquiring a closer knowledge of and esteem for his way of working and by loving him for himself.'

"Söderblom's sympathy for the principles of the

Labour movement grew still more during his last years at Paris. In the spring of 1899 he commented on a lockout of North Swedish sawyers who had refused to renounce their trade-union membership. 'It is quite clear that the trades-union movement is the only and best way to social security. Why aggravate its growing-pains by such drastic measures? This seems to me a unique opportunity for the clergy, headed by their bishop, to make their office fruitful in a fitting cause. By their position the clergy are given an enviable opportunity to help both parties to come to an understanding. What a pity to let such an opportunity pass unused!' "

A pity, indeed, that the actual course of events compelled Swedish Labour to make its own way without reference to the Church!

§

I supplement Bishop Andrae's record by some significant extracts from Söderblom's letters and addresses. In 1897 he hoped the Congress for the History of Religion would bring a revival among educated circles which were hitherto indifferent. From the International Socialist Congress in Paris of 1900 he gathers the impression of a powerful, youthful, and idealistic movement, displaying something of the enthusiasm and feeling of solidarity of the early Christians, and—except for evangelical Christianity—the only reassuring factor "in face of the really destructive forces in the contemporary world. May God give it good educators, so that it may go on from the merely economic problems where it began towards interest in all the high questions of life. May God give to the men of the Church wisdom and courage to apply Jesus's words, 'He that is not against us, is for us.' " In his memorable inaugural address to the students of divinity given at Uppsala in 1901, he congratulates them on being, under their Master, the proper peace-makers in the class war, the proper helpers of the weak and betrayed, not seeking power or party but the redemption of souls, having a secret confidant in every heart in so far as they serve Christ's cause.

In 1909 he invited a large gathering of strikers, complete with band, to his church, himself heading the procession from the People's House. First, by giving a detailed account of the church building itself, he painted a picture of the long tradition of Christian worship there: "Here learned and unlearned, renowned and unknown men, sought edification. Now it is our turn. Soon we shall have left our places and fresh hosts will come in after us." In this "breathless silence, this hour of tremendous devotion" (G. Kyhlberg) he went on to his subject proper—the Church in the light of religious history. He pointed out how Christianity had found Sweden with a firmly established tradition not of myths but of laws, as one would expect in a people always free: "Respect for law has characterized our people at all times. If we now should lose our respect for law, it would mean our going back in development for thousands of years." And he went on to show how the nation had grown up to decency, discipline and solidarity in the hard school of the Reformation, resulting in Gustavus Adolphus's vindication of religious freedom—"and, gentlemen, why should we not recognize a genius, even if he happens to be a king?" He ended by a spirited presentation of the characteristics of biblical religion: "Briefly they can be expressed by three words: *fire, forward, comfort*. The first means the burning demand for justice which already in the Prophets directs the *fire* of discontent against everything evil—primarily against the evil in man. The watchword of Western cultuie can be said to be *forward*. Forward—even through the death of the Cross! That is the idea of evolution—for evolution must never be conceived as a line continually rising automatically: it requires sacrifice and struggle. Yet in his forward striving the Christian recognizes his weakness, imperfection and guilt. Here comes in the third thing: *comfort*. It is the gift of forgiveness which conveys the real power of going forward."

Each can see for himself the deep love inspiring the speaker, which made him put forward everything that is alive in Christianity and able to be brought to life in his listeners, hard-bitten men of the continental-socialist type, apparently so far from Christianity yet guided by a loving mind and hand to look behind all artificial party divisions and walls. This is apologetics at its best: elastic yet unyielding, wholly constructive, and hinting at mysteries yet to be attained.

Here are briefly some further examples of Söderblom's life-long striving for the soul of socialism and the socialists. In 1913 he thinks of acquiring Keir Hardie as an Olaus Petri lecturer. In 1920, when the socialist leader Hjalmar Branting was seen in the gallery during the session of the Church Assembly discussing social problems, he succeeded in getting him on to the platform. Söderblom said on this occasion: "Those who do not stop at the surface have long realized the spirit of idealism and sacrifice which is the essence of your movement. What does the Church stand for, or ought she to stand for? I would say, for unselfish zeal, for justice, and for faith which is more than calculation. At this time we cannot afford unnecessary antagonisms and avoidable divisions."

Söderblom gave his first address after his return from his Gifford lectures in Scotland to a large youth meeting, during his last episcopal visitation of a parish, in June 1931. He talked about a Scottish miner, James Brown, M.P., an old champion of total abstinence and a Sunday-school teacher, who had said that "The Church of Scotland has made me what I am." "Mr. Brown seems to me to be living evidence for three propositions: No improvement of society can be achieved without the improvement of men; no improvement can be achieved through hatred, violence or anything of that kind; it can only be achieved when justice, truth, and love so penetrate a man that he becomes his own educator." When preaching his last sermon, a week before his passing, Söderblom said, "A Christian ought to exercise his influence not only in the divine service, not only through words, but also, as our Saviour and the apostles did, by means of his whole nature. Discipleship should be practised through a man's personality and his zeal exercised in all situations of life; and that can be attained only by having been weighed down by one's own impotence and put beneath God's living power."

Thus are we shown the urgent problems of social reconciliation in their true context of the still greater problem of a general renewal from above.

4

SÖDERBLOM'S struggle for peace between the nations also received its early impulse from his wrestling with Tolstoyan ideas in his Paris years. "He was deeply stirred by Tolstoy's protest against war. Tolstoy had 'awakened in Christianity its dormant sense of the horror of war and of the unchristian character of all power.' Custom had turned something most horrible and detestable into something quite natural. Our sense of the atrociousness of war has been dulled. 'If, beside Tolstoy's accusing reveille, you hear the representatives and protectors of the Church singing the praise of brute force on behalf of the Church, you are reminded of the old saying that the Church needs to learn Christianity from its adversaries.' Certainly the problem of peace is not to be solved by a turn of the hand. Yet the Christian Church must by no means cling to the idea that the present emergency is bound to last as long as the world. The time for peace can come; working and praying that this may happen is necessarily connected with Christian belief."

Yet, seriously as Söderblom took Tolstoy as a storm-signal, his own teaching in these years shows that, far from making Tolstoy's weak sentimentality his own, he took his stand firmly upon historic Christianity.

To Söderblom the innermost mystery of the life of Jesus was the mystery of the Redeemer listening to the Father's voice, fulfilling a divine call and putting it before his followers. In contrast also to Tolstoy's revolutionary attitude Jesus was to him the culmination of history, the fulfilment of promises centuries old, forming part of history and yet immediately forming fresh history which cannot be understood unless thorough account is taken of him.

"On November 8, 1914 there was an evening service in Uppsala cathedral. The newly-consecrated archbishop mounted the pulpit and spoke about the distress of the war and the Christian duty of assiduous prayer and endeavour to realize Christian brotherhood in a time of discord and hatred. 'The war cannot rend the ties with which Christ unites the faithful. Let us pray to the Lord that he may grant us peace, that the day may soon come when the nations may unite in love and Christ be lord of all, the day which will fulfil the prayers of the saints.' This was his first official act. Yet it was not the first time he had pleaded in favour of peace. In the autumn of 1905, when Norway broke the union with Sweden and the two countries were brought to the verge of war, Söderblom preached a sermon in which he thanked God that peace had been preserved in spite of everything, and laid upon his hearers the duty of addressing themselves without bitterness or looking backward to the tasks facing their own nation—a sermon which caused some offence and was criticized as a proof of national surrender. It was to the credit of Söderblom that the Scandinavian Student Christian Movement was held together.

"The cloud which the severing of the union had brought into the sky of peace in Scandinavia was as nothing compared with the twilight of the gods which in 1914 plunged the whole world into darkness. Christians were carried away by the hurricane of chauvinism. Prelates proclaimed, in the spirit of the Old Testament, a just war in the name of the Lord of Hosts: 'The Lord is with us, our enemies are his enemies.' The representatives of humanism either mocked or lamented the bankruptcy of Christianity. While others talked, Söderblom acted."

It was in those first years of the war, during the period of his indefatigable endeavours to gather his universal Christian peace conference mentioned above by Bishop Brilioth, that Söderblom's teaching about international understanding and peace on earth reached maturity, in a form in which he was able to keep it throughout his life, modified only slightly according to the changing political and religious situation. The goal before his vision, far from being a mere consequence of the secular, cultural development of mankind, was purely religious, flowing from the Bible, from the Old and the New Testament alike. What the prophets once prophesied is on the way to being fulfilled. Much has come true, but we must listen to their message afresh and do the clear will of God. There can be no genuine peace until the rule of law and justice, and an administration of justice consistent with God's will, has been achieved; and, according to the will of God as expressed in the biblical revelation, the circle of those recognizing and obeying this divine law is providentially bound to widen more and more, from tribe to state, from state to world-wide community.

Söderblom's presentation of the theological problems involved also has a tone quite his own. Certainly he shares the pessimistic view on man common to St. Paul, St. Augustine and Luther. But there is something more, transposing the whole presentation to a different key—his most vivid conception of the continued revelation of the Holy Spirit and of the new life with which it endows the faithful. He points out the impotence of the natural man only in order to give him the confidence necessary for a complete surrender to God's omnipotence and for him to receive from God the creative power which is the sign of man's regeneration. That is why, if we may continue a musical metaphor, his scale was so rich. He could take a realistic view about man without making him lose hope, at the same time pointing out and leading him to the loftiest peaks without concealing their real height. So he knew how to avoid gloomy pessimism on the one hand and superficial optimism on the other. His "incarnationalism," as he once called it, helped him to avoid both these dangers.

On Midsummer day 1917 Söderblom gave an address to the Swedish Peace Congress in Uppsala. Confronted with the immediate horrors of the first world war, he conceived the task of the Church in the work for peace as fourfold: "to strengthen belief in God's might; to strengthen the sanctity of law and see a Christian duty in its development in international relations; to fight selfishness in the name of the love of Christ; to revive and strengthen consciousness of the Church's universality and unity above national boundaries. As Christians we must see our failures and omissions in all these respects." As he said on another occasion, "Only Christianity can do this work. Spirituality must not keep aloof in aristocratic and autarkic seclusion. The spiritual man is not always kind-hearted, the kind-hearted man not always spiritual. In Christianity spirituality and kindliness are indissolubly united."

Here is an impression of how Söderblom could bring home a special point to a special circle. In his capacity of vice-chancellor of Uppsala University and speaking in French, he addressed the conference of the International Law Association on the Majesty of Law. Their endeavours to bring under the absolute domination of the majesty of law wider and wider spheres wrested from the domination of disorder and arbitrariness had, he said, an ally in the Scriptures and Christian doctrine, which considered the continuous extension of lawful order, in its capacity of assuring security and liberty, to be a divine achievement. Yet this body of law must have a soul: "Love is the fulfilling of the law." It would, he declared, be one of the primary aims of the next year's Stockholm church conference to strengthen in all men, by a more thorough and clear-sighted teaching on the brotherhood of the nations, the frame of mind that was required if international legislation was to be upheld by a congenial spirit within the nations themselves.

To build up this favourable attitude at every stage of age and education Söderblom exerted all his ingenuity. He was proud to be the first to have written in his little text-book for schools and confirmation-classes: "Just as law and justice prevent violence within the state, so ought law and justice to hold sway in the mutual relations of states and to prevent war. Christ's command of love must therefore penetrate individuals and nations. Thus will peace be established in the world. All individuals and all nations must strive after this goal to the best of their abilities," and "The love of one's own people and country must not be defiled by unfriendly feelings towards other nations."

§

Söderblom's last noble achievement is closely connected with the problem of peace. At Stockholm this had been dealt with seriously but with some restraint, for the man who did most for the formulation of the resolution in question, Bishop Brent (convener of the Lausanne Conference on Faith and Order), rightly emphasized that the problem was not yet mature. The following years led further. They saw the hopes roused by the Locarno agreements and their breakdown. Over against the rising shadow of future fatal events there was the series of Kellogg pacts, agreements between nations renouncing war and introducing the idea of compulsory arbitration. Now the time was ripe for a word from the churches, pledging themselves to act as a body through their mouthpiece created by the Stockholm Conference, the 'Oecumenical Council.' Here again Söderblom can be said to have given a powerful impulse, by his Burge Memorial lecture in London, in the June of

1929, on the Church and Peace, summing up a life-long experience in the light of the new developments of those days. It was then that he first heard about the planned oecumenical pronouncement, but when the continuation committee of "Life and Work" met at Eisenach in September 1929 he was seriously ill and unable to be present. The resolution adopted there was drafted and submitted by the Bishop of Chichester, supported by Dr. Walter Simons and Professor Wilfred Monod, with a view to asking "This committee of the Universal Christian Conference to go as far as secular governments have already gone in endorsing the Kellogg Pact for the pacific settlement of disputes; and then to invite the churches to draw the logical conclusion from such action as churches. Its first paragraph hails the Kellogg Pact as a very great event and a landmark on the road to peace, repeating the essential words of the pact itself. The second repeats the conclusion reached by the committee of the Stockholm Conference. The third refers to the need of revising existing treaties in the interest of peace. The fourth is the crucial paragraph: it asks the churches to declare solemnly in unmistakable terms that they will not countenance any war, or encourage their countrymen to serve in any war, with regard to which the government of their country has refused an offer to submit the dispute to arbitration."

This resolution was approved by the World Alliance for Promoting Friendship through the Churches at Avignon in 1930, and was passed to the churches for endorsement. The Lambeth Conference of the Anglican communion made it its own by adopting its resolution 27 in 1930. And the same was achieved by Archbishop Söderblom at a general assembly of the Church of Sweden in 1931. On the three first points there was unanimity, but on the last the other bishops voted for a wording which, to Söderblom's mind, missed the point of the matter. It was hard for traditional

Lutheran feeling even to imagine an established church opposing the state on the state's own ground. Söderblom, on the contrary, held that the time for mere remonstrances had gone by. He even sharpened the wording, prefixing what we have seen to be his way of seeing the matter: "The rule of law is God's work, and it is the duty of the Church to inculcate its sanctity and to work for its building up even over the frontiers of nations." And he formulated the duty of the Church in case of disagreement with the government responsible thus: "When a state has undertaken with another state or several other states a general responsibility of submitting any disputes that arise to settlement, arbitration, or lawful decision, the Church must in every circumstance emphasize the binding nature of such an obligation, and therefore if in a given case the government of its own country, ignoring this obligation, declines to submit the dispute to such procedure, express its condemnation of every war that starts in this way and, in word and deed, dissociate itself from it."

In an article paving the way for the adoption of the resolution he ended by saying: "I wish only to emphasize that there is question of two loyalties. On the one hand loyalty towards a government which is breaking agreements solemnly pledged according to constitutional rules and starting a war of aggression; and on the other hand, loyalty towards international order and obligation. If I interpret rightly the meaning of the Scriptures and our confessions, the case is clear: the Church must not hesitate. She must speak out clearly and definitely. In the confession of sin of the Church of England there is confessed first that, 'We have left undone those things which we ought to have done,' and afterwards, 'We have done those things which we ought not to have done.' Sins of omission are condemned by Christ with equal emphasis with those of commission. As Christians, we ought at least to unite in pointing to the betterment of the heart and to the divine King's way of law. The rule of law is never complete. It suffers from imperfections which are sometimes crying. Yet the fact that a rule of law exists is, according to the Scriptures, the will of God. The continued extension of law is a continuation of God's creation. Here and now we must emphasize the sanctity of law with all our might, even if a heavy conflict should ensue."

When invited to speak on Armistice day 1930 Söderblom took as his subject the question, "Is the idea of peace an illusion?" and ended by saying: "It is our human and Christian call faithfully and patiently to work for what seems impossible (Matthew xix, 26), for peace, believing in God's promises, obeying his commandment. On the broad way, where a man leaves his self-sufficiency and his wicked passions 'at peace,' there is no peace to be found. Only at the strait gate, where a man does not leave himself 'at peace' but wages an irreconcilable war against the old Adam in himself and others, is there a way leading to peace."

In his last years Söderblom used every platform available for the promotion of peace on earth, ranging from the American Federal Council Bulletin of February 1929 to a speech in German over the Cologne radio in 1931. Thus he spent every ounce of his vanishing strength to try to check the deterioration in the world situation which was destined to issue in the lamentable failure of the often postponed disarmament conference. He did not live to see this failure. How he was missed when in 1937 the Oxford Conference on Church, Community and State drew up its resolution on the Church and peace! Was the Church, which had set its task so splendidly high at Eisenach, about to duck under the harder winds for the present? For among all the careful considerations and statements of that Oxford conference there was not a word about the Church, as such, giving a lead to the faithful in the hour of danger and deciding on their behalf, on her own authority, whether a war was unavoidable and therefore to be countenanced by the Church or not. Everything was left to the judgement of individual Christians, although it ought to have been clear that individuals are bound to lack some of the means necessary for judging so critical a situation. Yet there is no doubt that the higher standard reached in 1929 will be attained anew when the terrific waves of the present are stayed and fresh experience has added fresh strength and trust in God to those who long for a peace after God's mind.

§

There is, however, one field in which the seed so lavishly sown by Söderblom, far from being washed away, has lately sprouted wonderfully. His life-long effort to gather all sections of his nation around the God-given blessings of national freedom and Christian civilization, often judged as illusory and remote from reality, has reached a posthumous success amid the storms and anxieties of the present hour. I quote a striking illustration from *The Christian News-Letter*, No. 119 (February 4, 1942): "At the time of the meeting of the Swedish Church Assembly last November arrangements were made for a joint meeting, which is without precedent, between this supreme legislative body of the Swedish Church and the Swedish Parliament which was sitting at the same time. The joint meeting issued a statement to the Swedish nation urging it to stand unitedly and immovably for national freedom and Christian civilization. The pronouncement, which bore the personal signatures of the members of the two bodies, reads as follows:

" 'To the Swedish nation! All Swedish men and women 'in this time of violence and disunity are convinced 'that Swedish unity must be deepened and our freedom 'must remain untouched. With this in view, nothing is 'more necessary than that our nation should reconsider 'its task of carrying on the Christian civilization in-'herited from our fathers. We of the Parliament and 'Church Assembly gathered in the capital at this fateful 'hour for our country have therefore unanimously 'desired to recall our nation to our common heritage 'and our common responsibility. Sweden's line is the 'Christian line.' "

Does not this read like a fulfilling of Söderblom's keenest thoughts[1] and boldest prayers? Does not this growing seed, sown in hope against hope as it were, yet in complete obedience to God's clear commands, testify to the truth of God's ways and inspire hope everywhere, however much storms may still hinder us from lifting our heads in hope and our minds and hands to do the work pleasing to God?

---

[1] "*The nations are archangels,* created to practise God's commands, every tribe and every nation according to its gifts and its call. Nobody else can fill the task allotted to a certain nation" (in a letter to Lady Ailsa).

5

MY most difficult task is to give, in a limited space, some small impressions of the abundance of memorial literature about Söderblom. The comprehensive range of the contributors is amazing: more than 180 authors, from twenty-four nations, put down their impressions on over 3,000 pages. Their contributions vary from a book to a few pages of simple reminiscence. Among them are sixty Swedes and six members of the Swedish Lutheran Augustana Synod in U.S.A., four Finns, five Danes, six Norwegians, seventeen British, twelve Germans (including some Roman Catholics), and eight Americans. From the Swedish Crown Prince, who voiced the pride of Sweden when addressing the inhabitants of Söderblom's native place, to the village churchwarden who told how Söderblom during a visitation himself climbed through the church roof into the loft and there discovered some forgotten treasures of ecclesiastical art, from the court of the Bishop of Iceland to Albert Schweitzer's tropical hospital in Lambarene and the mission station in China, contributors unite in their homage. Here we see reflected the spirit of a man who from his youth cultivated friendship as a sacrament, pointing to Luther's saying in the Smalcaldic Articles that there is a sacrament of *mutuum colloquium et fraterna consolatio*.

From his student years onwards there were bonds of friendship severed only by death. The international youth conferences at Northfield (1890) and Amsterdam (1891), where the brilliant promise of the Swedish student were recognized by both Scandinavians and others, provided him with friends who later on became his most faithful and inspiring collaborators, men such as John Mott and Lyder Brun and Wilfred Monod, perhaps the most congenial of them all. In a short talk, on a Basel railway-platform, he won the president of the Reich court of appeal, Dr. W. Simons, to his great cause for life.

He intervened decisively in the life of many people, both as their helper and as a furtherer of the great common task. As a professor he lifted his students to a higher level by showing confidence in their abilities and by setting them hard tasks. In general, his way was to set high aims before them and then to leave them on their own to pursue their course. Professor J. Hempel tells how he was compelled to learn English in six weeks so as to be able to report on an English publication to Söderblom's seminar.

What he required from others, he did himself. Henry A. Atkinson tells how Söderblom insisted on consecrating Bishop Kukk in Tallinn in the Estonian language, Bishop Irbe records his astonishment at being consecrated in Latvian, Professor Žilka testifies that at Prague the archbishop in giving a lecture on the connections between Sweden and Bohemia used the Czech tongue, after only a short time of preparation—and all of them recollect how well he acquitted himself in these languages. This Söderblom thought to be a duty of international courtesy, and would give friendly rebukes on the subject in his inimitable way: at the oecumenical meeting in Copenhagen in 1922 Bishop Ammundsen heard him proposing in jest a resolution that Americans should not be forbidden to learn foreign languages!

S. Gabrielsson, well-known in England, who had suffered a humiliation as a young priest, was given an Olaus Petri exhibition and enabled to make studies in England which later proved to be of great consequence. Dr. Herman Neander, too, was sent to Greece in order to become acquainted with the Eastern Orthodox Church in all its branches: everybody knows—he tells the story in a brilliant book—what that meant for the incorporation into the oecumenical movement of the Eastern churches and for charitable activity during the war of 1914-18 among Russian prisoners-of-war in Germany and Germans in Russia and Siberia. There are other points of the highest interest in Dr. Neander's book, *e.g.*, what he has to say about Söderblom's serious attempt to hold the door open even to Soviet Russia.

So, too, he rescued researchers brought to the verge of desperation by war and its privations. It is moving to read Albert Schweitzer's report—at Christmas 1919 he was living at Strassburg, without any hope of resuming his medical activity in Lambarene. Söderblom, who had thought him to be a prisoner, invited him to give lectures in Uppsala and procured a publisher for his lectures on ethics; he arranged a circular tour of Sweden, so that Schweitzer should clear off by organ-recitals the heavy debts he had incurred in his missionary work; he caused him to write his famous book about Lambarene, by prompting a Swedish publisher to take the risk, and, in this way, got him the means to begin again in Africa. Söderblom helped many in similar ways—I just mention another theologian, from the opposite side, Nikolay Glubokovsky, whom he twice enabled to leave bolshevik Russia. This aged scholar, thus helped to many a year of teaching and oecumenical activity, confesses that "After the death of my younger friend I have felt fatherless in my old age."

Opportunity for thus helping others was given in a wonderful way. One day in 1908 a lady, unknown to him thitherto and unknown to the public to this day, offered Söderblom 80,000 crowns for the furtherance of theological studies, which gave rise to the Olaus Petri Foundation.

The same spontaneous goodness, understanding and encouragement expressed itself also in the most humble acts of service. Nearly all the memorial contributors who stayed with him tell how Söderblom carried their bags to and from the station, in spite of his age, weak heart and position. He would carry a washing-basket for an old woman, and help to push a wheelbarrow up the hill near the archbishop's house. People in Uppsala gave him the nickname "Porter No. 13." The most simple Salvation-Army private was as sure to be well received and helped as any high dignitary. He made every human spirit ring true; and after his death their sound blends together in a symphonic undertone.

§

In this symphony of various voices an abundance of the deepest questions is argued. Söderblom's daring initiative, moving heaven and earth, is unanimously praised, but it is equally shown that he could keep himself in the background when he thought it right for the sake of the common cause. The northern primates agree that in this way he made it easy for them to dispel in their churches the natural suspicion of an intended predominance. Bishop Ostenfeld of Copenhagen calls him a "most loyal colleague. Although he did all the correspondence work, I know nobody more loyal and considerate towards his collaborators." In the second conference of northern bishops, Bishop J. Helgason of Iceland observed that "At any rate he showed not the least inclination to play the leading part; he seemed rather by his bearing to strive to avoid such an idea of himself." Professor Aalders of Groningen had the same impression at Lausanne in 1927. This was in accordance with Söderblom's inmost nature: "He was never in the least conceited, but retained his downright straightforwardness, the child in him remained alive throughout his whole life and activity" (Ostenfeld). "The sons of God are free" (The Bishop of Chichester). He was "a soul of crystal" (H. Monnier, quoting Victor Hugo). "Being himself sincere and true, a convincing impression of personal genuineness was always the decisive thing for him" (Lyder Brun). His effect on others was "enriching, not oppressive" (Bishop Irbe). "His organic insight into religious history and his Christocentric orientation towards life had been developed into what was the most charming thing in his whole rich personality, the fruitful sense of solidarity in face of all living things. He was rich in God. Therefore were his oecumenical interests so genuine, and therefore could he tolerate opposition and mistrust" (K. L. Reichelt, the founder and leader of the Norwegian Buddhist Mission in East Asia). He represented "a synthesis of nature and grace" (Professor Pröhle-Sopron). "His distinction was entirely moral, his authority entirely spiritual, and both were real" (M. J. Viénot).

Not simply his manifold talent but "perhaps his irresistible simple Christian personality, dominating by means of its convincing power, is one of the greatest gifts which through him were given to the world. He was reported to be ambitious. We can truly say: Above all he was dedicated to a cause, the service of which did not tolerate personal ambition" (Charles Macfarland). "In his student years and through his whole life he had a rare faculty of setting in motion the inmost depths of the hearts of others. If it is true, as has been said by a distinguished Indian civil servant, that we rule with our hearts, we can understand something of Söderblom's ability to gain and to persuade people which he showed himself to possess in an increasing degree in difficult and important, even critical, negotiations, when persons holding opposite views were to be united" (John Mott). "He could not have become the man he was, rich, noble, living, human, if he had not spent himself unsparingly whenever he felt himself called to do so. Everything he accomplished was an answer to some crying need, and the impulse he gave to the Protestant Church in Europe and America in its entirety was impressively strong" (David S. Cairns). "When confronted by a great task, demanding the

F

utmost exertion of all his gifts and power, he placed himself entirely at its disposal, and it was edifying to see how his inner man grew as he gave himself. This is, as it were, his last will and testament, the obligation which he quietly and seriously imposed upon his associates" (Professor Nörregaard, Copenhagen).

"Of all his gifts none was so wonderful and so unforgettable as that of holding the key to the hearts of men. He knew how to gain the confidence of a depressed sceptic of the highest culture, such as Alfred Nobel, as well as the heart of a despairing Swedish sea-captain whom he found on a boat, when his archiepiscopal visitation of the Swedish congregation at Copenhagen even included the ships in the harbour. The case seemed hopeless: Söderblom mastered it and, on his way back, he asked the Swedish seamen's pastor, 'Is there any happiness comparable with that which we experience when it is given us to help to heal wounds of the heart?' " (M. Neiiendam). "His leadership depended not only on his richness in ideas and on his prophetic faculty of forming spiritual perspectives, but also on his faith in the cause itself, which drew all others after him. It was God's cause. It could only be furthered by penitent, praying and believing hands. Söderblom tried always to safeguard the spiritual character of the movement, to keep it alive as a defiant and daring enterprise of faith in difficult times" (Adolf Keller). "His greatest life-work was born of the deepest trouble, from the pains of his vicarious suffering" (Paul le Seur). "No great achievement happens here below in the moral and religious sphere without a man giving it his whole soul and finally dedicating his whole life to it" (Wilfred Monod).

"In Söderblom Protestantism got a real leader for the first time since its rise. It was an achievement which cannot be overrated that he understood that the time had come for the Protestant churches to collaborate and to shape a common church. The man who ventured to assert this idea universally had nothing to rely on, besides the personal authority with which he could put it forward, but the power of persuasion represented by the idea. . . . His success is due to the spirit emanating from him and influencing his surroundings: this spirit triumphed—because the personality from which it emanated was so unselfish. Yet in the last resort the great power he exerted over men was founded on his deep and simple piety, which continuously gained new power to bestow on others. Seldom, except when he preached or led prayers, have I heard him express his piety in words: words were superfluous—one sensed it, his whole nature was full of it. When conversation turned upon spiritual matters, his piety would find immediate expression. In such moments he found words of such devoutness that in his presence one felt pervaded by the breath of eternity" (Albert Schweitzer). In Geneva in 1920 "some one had dwelt on the difficulties and had said that one might hope that time would smooth them down. Thereupon Söderblom asked, 'What is it we believe in? Is it in Time or in God?' This cleared the air and put pessimism to flight" (Dr. Karl Fries). "This daring springs from his heart and conscience. And this is just the mysterious charity by which this noble Scandinavian champion of Evangelical and social Catholicism has won us over. . . . He has obeyed the supernatural reason which spoke louder in his conscience than all reasoning. This is why we, his friends, love him' (Elie Gounelle).

§

He was a great joy-bringer. Whether a disheartened student or oecumenical colleagues, they unanimously relate how, for example, a common railway journey with Söderblom freed them from tiredness and depression. When Bishop Ammundsen returned from "C.O.P.E.C." in 1924, feeling ill, tired and depressed, he met Söderblom between London and Harwich. "The journey took on an entirely altered complexion because he was with me. He gave, as it were, an injection of courage and power." The same is said by Alfred Th. Jörgensen, also a Dane, back in 1892, when Söderblom and he were still students. "The circle of those to whom he became God's messenger of joy grew wider and wider until it included the whole of Christendom. We see how wide this circle was if we consider not only the progressive development of his work but also how he found time to be a messenger of joy in small things, to all those with whom he came into contact, by encouraging words or helpful deeds in their special difficulties. I sometimes ask myself whether the greatest and most enduring aspect of his achievement does not lie in the seed which he sowed in this way, as it were in passing" (Bishop Einar Billing).

Söderblom exercised the double art of making himself understood and of unsealing other men's lips. But "in his nature he combined contrasts which are not generally found in the same person. He had a straightforward manner which took men by storm and made friends all over the world, but at the same time he was extremely reticent about himself and allowed nobody to come too near. He seemed to me to be a lonely man, and I have often wondered whether among all his friends he had any—except his wife—who was his true confidant, who really knew him. He was a keen optimist who roused a joy in work, and there was hopefulness wherever he came, but at the same time he knew the anxiety and troubles of the human heart, the dark depths of the soul. . . . He could appear to fritter away his energy in a bewildering variety of undertakings, yet he had only a few pronounced aims in all his activity. He could give the impression of being distracted by a day's tasks, yet he concentrated on essentials to an astonishing degree. He could be overwhelmed by work and hurried by excitement, but within his soul quietness ruled" (Folke Palmgren, chaplain to the archbishop during the years of the Stockholm Conference). "Were there not many things in him which remained hidden? Yes, certainly. Where and for whom should he have released his overflowing power?—he who at every moment was filled with overflowing life! A Niagara, a cataract!" (E. Tennmann, Dorpat). "Was not the archbishop, in spite of all his communicativeness and openheartedness, one of the most reticent of men? To how many did he unlock the doors of the secret chamber and workshop of his life? Had he not his cross? Who was with him in his Gethsemane, who in his hours of transfiguration? The moment of his death lifted him into a new glory before our eyes" (C. G. Friman). "How much bitterness—not suppressed, but overcome—there was behind the charm which Nathan Söderblom had acquired apparently so easily nobody, even in his immediate circle, can say. But the joy he brought, and will a long time after his death continue to bring, to our joyless age does not become less if his song should prove to be 'born of sorrow,' as the Swedish hymn says" (Lydia Wahlström).

Bishop Rodhe of Lund reminds us of another great Swedish archbishop, J. O. Wallin (d.1839), the creator of the Swedish hymnary of 1819, who, like Söderblom, so appealed to the imagination: "He also was a man who allowed himself no rest from work. But his restlessness, as one can guess, was not caused by mere delight in working. He had by unrestrained activity to subdue the demons of melancholy gnawing his life's nerve. Söderblom spoke much about the Cross, especially after his activity began to extend over the world, when he became well-known, when more honours were showered upon him than on any other Swede. Perhaps he has more points of contact with Wallin than one is inclined at first to believe, but nevertheless the total impression which Söderblom makes is quite different.

Some time ago I talked about him to one of our cultural leaders. 'Christianity has its shining and its dark and burdensome aspect, and both of them are justified,' he said. 'But never have I met a man who, in spite of all, brought out its shining aspect as did Söderblom.' That is the picture of him that lives in countless hearts."

On November 8, 1939, the twenty-fifth anniversary of the day when Söderblom was consecrated archbishop, a bronze bust of him was unveiled at the deanery of Uppsala University. His successor, Archbishop Eidem, made a memorial speech, taking as his text St. John i, 45–51, about the vocation of Nathanael, the text of the sermon at his consecration. Since this speech is a most competent and up-to-date testimony a passage from it may appropriately close this series of estimates of Söderblom's character.

> "To-day, when we celebrate the unforgettable memory of Archbishop Söderblom, I wish to dwell in grateful homage on three words which may be especially applied to him, *viz.*, 'Come and see,' 'Heaven open,' and 'Greater things.' 'Come and see'; this characterized him and his whole vision of life. In his activity both in research and as a leader he wished to build upon the foundation of experience. He was always strongly opposed to all that was conventional and to all that he could not verify himself. It was experience of life that he wished to know and to build upon. The next trait characterizing Nathan Söderblom was the glad and open profession of something above, of something not belonging to this world: 'Heaven open.' The third trait was an unbroken 'excelsior,' a longing for 'Greater things,' an endeavour never to halt at a goal attained, a continuous endeavour upward and onward. These three traits were characteristic of three of the offices of his life, those of teacher, leader and disciple. . . . Nathan

Söderblom was great as a teacher and as a leader; but he was greatest as a disciple of the great master, our Lord Jesus Christ, and this is the greatest thing one can say about any man."

§

The mass of memorial literature naturally contains many single features which give important clues for the understanding of Söderblom, and, moreover, much valuable material for church history, of which some is known to the closer circle of oecumenical leaders but some other may be new and important. The English reader may appreciate reading what Lady Parmoor testifies from the dark year 1917: "Owing to war restrictions we could not assemble for several years, but the power of the personality of the archbishop was so great that his letters became a source of inspiration for our whole work. When it did not prove feasible for British citizens to follow the archbishop's invitation to visit Sweden, we arranged meetings in England and created spiritual ties, being absent bodily, but present spiritually. It was the strong faith of Archbishop Söderblom which rendered such a thing possible and which gave to the collaborators such an experience which they will never forget. They will remember him as the prophet of Christian Unity."

At the "C.O.P.E.C." conference Söderblom did all he could to set the German delegates free from their depressing sense of persistent isolation after the end of the war. He suggested to Sir Henry Lunn that he should invite Baron von Pechmann to dinner. How right Söderblom was can be seen from the words spoken by Baron von Pechmann later on in the evening: "I wish you could see into my heart to-night and realize how this conversation has poured balm into my soul." "Events like this made possible the great oecumenical meeting in Stockholm in 1925, when

Frenchmen, Germans and Englishmen met at a conference for the first time after the world war," concludes Sir Henry.

During the last war Charles Macfarland came to France, attached to the American army as a non-combatant, leading a movement for the rebuilding of the Protestant churches devastated by the war. Invited to come to Sweden as an Olaus Petri lecturer, he had to decline, as Söderblom was mistrusted because of his connections with German Christians. Yet "the same French church leader who then had hinted that the archbishop was producing propaganda in favour of Germany, later on became his warm admirer and sat with him in fraternal deliberations."

The man who in 1926 spontaneously joined the Swiss choir in Berne and assisted with his tenor voice, to whom crowds of people cried *"auf Wiedersehen"* in Stuttgart in 1921, was equal to such a task as is described by Lyder Brun, namely, the address given in 1930 at the banquet in Oslo after the presentation of the Nobel peace prize to Mr. Kellogg and himself. It was "an address which certainly no one else could have given at such a juncture as this; full of personal recollections and observations, now merry, now as serious as a sermon, and, with the rich variety of his sudden flashes of thought and happy anecdotes, able to turn this highly official assembly of most heterogeneous persons into a sort of happy family. Thus the effect of the address was expressively defined by a foreign diplomat present who had not understood much of what was said, but who had observed to his astonishment the humours this wizard of an archbishop had been able to conjure up, swaying his hearers from merriment to inspiration or deep devoutness."

There is strikingly consistent evidence concerning Söderblom's belief in life after death, important because in 1928 his account of the Resurrection was attacked as being "modernistic." Once in Heaven he would meet and speak to whomsoever he wished. He said to H. A. Atkinson,

"When I get to Heaven, I shall go to see Tertullian, Athanasius and some more of them, and we shall have time to elucidate much that I have wished to know during my whole life." On another occasion, when we were talking about the Patriarch Photios of Alexandria, he said, "Another privilege I shall have in Heaven will be to converse with Clement concerning the problems he had to solve in his time." Professor K. G. Westman relates a dialogue between himself and Söderblom whose starting point was a little book of the archbishop's in honour of his friend Dr. S. A. Fries. In it Söderblom had written that "Sam Fries rejoices in Heaven." Interviewed, Söderblom firmly maintained his belief in his deceased friend's real participation in what was said after his death regarding the questions interesting him in his life-time. Whilst granting that our Lord had not revealed the details of his purposes, Söderblom ended by saying, "I only can say as my personal testimony that I very often perceive that my own father follows from Heaven what I am doing and planning." In a memorial letter about his Finnish friend Professor A. H. Hjelt, he writes to Bishop Gummerus of Tampere: "We are connected by ties ever more and more spiritual with those near and dear to us, because they have passed on to the other world in which our intercourse shall continue for ever." And a distinguished old lady parishioner from his Paris congregation wrote to Sweden, after having passed an evening with the Söderbloms, "Pastor Söderblom, who is not fanatical in any way, says he would not live one more day if he had not the hope that we are not done with in this life."

§

The following is a record of some points of interest for church historians, arranged in chronological order.

The late Archbishop Davidson of Canterbury used to

speak to Swedish friends about his repeated attempts to get into touch with the Archbishop of Uppsala in 1888 in order to foster closer relations between the two churches. Although provided with an introductory letter from his father-in-law, Archbishop Tait of Canterbury, he did not succeed in being received by Archbishop Niklas Sundberg: "It was clear that he did not wish to see me and that he was not interested in a closer relation between our churches." Samuel Gabrielsson repeats Söderblom's suggested explanation for this discourtesy: "Sundberg had a weakness for inflicting himself upon people, and when it was impossible for him to do this, he preferred to stay in the background. Now he could not speak English, and he may have felt ashamed to use an interpreter, and this may be the explanation for his negative attitude." The same article records the joy with which, in 1893, the telegram of congratulation on the occasion of the anniversary of the Uppsala Synod of 1593, which established the Church of Sweden, was received by those students of theology who, compared with their professors, held a more modern view of theology; for the congratulatory message of Archbishop Benson of Canterbury expressed his hope that the word of God, *studied in the full light of modern research*, might be a benediction. This weighted the balance against the traditionalism in theological views then ruling.

Gabrielsson also relates that Bishop Tottie, who paid an official visit to the Lambeth Conference of 1908, representing the Church of Sweden, had refused the request of the Swedish archbishop to make this visit and only agreed when officially ordered to go by his king. Söderblom was rightly amazed at this. He said to Gabrielsson, "What do the Anglican bishops care for his Majesty of Sweden! What impresses them is that a messenger comes from the Church of Sweden who presents a message from the Archbishop of Uppsala." This letter of salutation in Latin was provided by

Söderblom; but Archbishop Ekman, a scrupulous man of saintly character, thought it necessary to correct it as a matter of conscience, because its classical Latin was better than any he could have produced.

From the first Continental Conference for Home Missions, held at Munich in 1922, Professor K. B. Westman relates two incidents. At a Roman Catholic meeting in Munich, Cardinal Archbishop Faulhaber had criticized the Treaty of Versailles for being "popeless." In his famous sermon on the Samaritan who himself now needed help, Söderblom said, without any controversial intent, that this treaty was bad because it was "neighbourless." The only British participator in the conference, Dr. Alexander Ramsay, itinerant secretary of the Word Alliance, sat at the side of a German who asked him to share his hymnal. Ramsay was somewhat astonished when he learnt later on that the friendly gentleman was General Ludendorff—whose aversion from Christianity was seen only later.

Dr. Brandelle, former president of the American-Swedish Lutheran Augustana Synod, records from the Lutheran world convention held at Eisenach in 1923: "Certainly there were people who were not at all pleased that Söderblom participated in the conference, and secret attempts were made to shut him out. The American delegation boycotted these attempts. The opposition dwindled away, and the general feeling was that the archbishop was more welcome than anybody else."

It is well-known that the report of the seventh commission of the Lausanne Conference, submitted by Söderblom, was rejected. The passages in it, opposed by a small American minority, were not even written by Söderblom, but the opposition aimed at him. It was a fine act of chivalry when the true author of these passages, Charles F. d'Arcy, former archbishop of Armagh, wrote: "When he was the president of the noted seventh commission, Söderblom made use of his vision and won appreciation of it by all its members. . . . He combined with his personal power of persuasion and influence a generosity in views which created a particularly good impression. One could have wished that the conference had followed his example as a whole. . . . I am even persuaded that decisive and especially important steps could have been taken at Lausanne if the spirit and the purposes of Söderblom could have gained the victory over the narrower points of view maintained by certain other people."

An American missionary to India, Dr. John Banninga, tells us what great help the Church of Sweden has rendered to the Indian free churches in the difficult negotiations concerning the South India scheme of church union. Later on he says, "The Church of Sweden, in preserving the apostolic tradition both in succession and church customs and at the same time remaining throughout evangelical, may lead the way for those churches which will now attempt to base a church union on a constitutional episcopate which will grant full freedom to the evangelical tendency as well as to high-church views." Banninga's judgement of the Lausanne Conference corresponds with that of Archbishop d'Arcy.

§

This choir of memorial writers has this stirring and continuing effect on our ears—each contributor provides one aspect of Söderblom's life. But at the same time there is something else behind each contribution. Presenting themselves, they present the finest aspects of their own lives as influenced by the archbishop. They beckoned us to take our place, and we have blended our voices in a harmony in which the results of Nathan Söderblom's master-touch may still be heard.

BIBLIOGRAPHY

1. Two Swedish biographies appeared as early as 1931, a short popular one by Olle Nystedt and another by Tor Andrae. Andrae's biography is a rich source and should not be overlooked by those interested in the spiritual currents of the time. These have both been translated into German, but the latter in an abbreviated and otherwise inadequate form. In 1933 Michael Neiiendam published a short Danish biography. There is a very good biographical sketch in English by Yngve Brilioth, prefixed to Söderblom's posthumous Gifford lectures *The Living God*, London, 1933.

2. *Hågkomster och livsintryck* ("Memoirs and Impressions"). Edited by Sven Thulin. 3 volumes. Uppsala, 1931, 1931, 1934.

Eivind Berggrav: *Nathan Söderblom—Geni og Karakter* ("Genius and Character"). Oslo, 1931.

Herman Neander: *Med Nathan Söderblom—Krigsfångevård och ekumenisk gärning* ("Care for Prisoners of War and Oecumenical Action"). Stockholm, 1932.

Special numbers of *Kristen Gemenskap* (ed. N. Karlström), October, 1931, and *Eine heilige Kirche* (ed. Fr. Heiler), 1931, Nos. 9-10; 1936, Nos. 5-6.

Mgr. Nathan Söderblom, Archevêque d'Upsal; Sa Personne, Son Œuvre, Sa Pensée. Discours prononcés par MM. les Professeurs J. Viénot, H. Monnier, W. Monod à la Faculté libre de Théologie protestante de Paris, le 15 décembre 1931. Paris, 1932.

Michael Neiiendam: *Nathan Söderblom*. Kjöbenhavn, 1933.

Knut B. Westman: *Minnestal över Nathan Söderblom* ("Memorial Speech on N. S."). Stockholm, 1934.

3. *Nathan Söderblom: In Memoriam.* By Tor Andrae, Gustaf Aulén, Manfred Björkquist, Yngve Brilioth, Gunnar Dahlquist, Bengt Jonzon, Emil Liedgren and Sven Ågren. Edited by Nils Karlström; a preface by Einar Billing. Stockholm, 1931.

4. Nils Karlström: *Från Northfield till Stockholm: Till den ekumeniska tankens historia i Ärkebiskop Söderbloms liv* ("From Northfield to Stockholm: Materials for the History of the Development of N. S.'s Oecumenical Thought, collected from his early Diaries and Letters").

Folke Holmström: *Nathan Söderbloms självbiografiska uttalanden om umgdomsårens avgörande kriser. Dokument* ("Autobiographical Allusions to the Decisive Crises of his Early Years, collected from N. S.'s published and unpublished papers"). *Svensk Teologisk Kvartalsskrift*, 1935, No. 4.

5. Folke Holmström: *Uppenbarelsereligion och Mystik: En undersökning av Nathan Söderbloms teologi* ("Mysticism and the Religion of Revelation: An investigation of the Theology of N. S."). Stockholm, 1937. This has been reviewed in English in *The Augustana Quarterly*, April, 1939.

The following is a preparatory study: Folke Holmström: *Bidrag till Nathan Söderbloms Bibliografi: Textkritiska Prolegomena till metodisk Söderblomforskning* ("Contributions to a Bibliography of N.S.: The Textual Criticism of Söderblom's works as a Clue to the Understanding of his Theology"). Lund, 1937, reprinted from *Svensk Teologisk Kvartalsskrift*.

J. M. van Veen: *Nathan Söderblom, Leven en Denken van een Godsdiensthistoricus* ("Life and Thought of a Religious Historian"). Amsterdam, 1940.

Nils Karlström: *Kristna Samförståndssträvanden under Världskriget 1914–18* ("Christian Movements for Fellowship during the War of 1914–1918"). Stockholm, 1947.

This important work gives much new information about Söderblom, recorded by his chaplain.

6. Peter Katz: *Nathan Söderblom, Ein Führer zu kirchlicher Einheit* ("A Leader in the Movement for Church Unity"). Halle a/S, 1925.

7. Peter Katz: *Nathan Söderbloms schriftstellerisches Werk: Versuch eines Ueberblicks* ("N. S.'s Literary Activity: An attempt to Survey his Published Works." *Die Eiche*, ed. Fr. Siegmund-Schultze, 1933, 1.).

www.ingramcontent.com/pod-product-compliance
Lightning Source LLC
Chambersburg PA
CBHW070323100426
42743CB00011B/2528

9 781532 686092